NW

BIRDS

OF ANGLIAN WATER RESERVOIRS

Written by John And⌐
Illustrated by Mike La⌐

Foreword by the Royal Society
for the Protection of Birds

Anglian Water

AN ANGLIAN WATER GUIDE

Published by Anglian Water plc, Anglian House,
Ambury Road, Huntingdon, Cambridgeshire. PE18 6NZ

80 000 614 958

Northamptonshire
Libraries

598 . 2942

NW
1/93

Published by Anglian Water plc, Anglian House,
Ambury Road, Huntingdon, Cambridgeshire

This edition published 1992
© Copyright Anglian Water 1992

ISBN 0 9519816 0 9

Printed by Stanley L. Hunt (Printers) Ltd, Rushden.

Contents

Acknowledgements

Anglian Water warmly thanks all those who have helped in the preparation of this guide. Particular thanks are due to John Andrews (until recently Chief Conservation Advisor with the RSPB) who prepared most of the text and to Mike Langman for his excellent bird illustrations.

Other major contributors included members of the Anglian Water conservation team. Particular acknowledgement is due to Nina Sage who provided much of the text on operational and leisure aspects of the reservoirs. Paul Woodcock contributed introductory text and, assisted by Nina Sage, oversaw development of the project. Kevin Hewston also supplied text and Andrew Snelson assisted with proof reading. Thanks are also due to Julie Silk of the Anglian Water Public Relations team and to Nell Game of The Art Company for the production of the Guide.

Special thanks are owed to those who provided bird data. These include J. Glasebrook (Alton), R. Moss (Cadney), A. Harding (Caldecotte & Willen), P. Milford (Costessey), K. Wilson (Covenham), D. Roberts (Foxcote), R. Porter (Grafham), R. Bullock (Hollowell, Pitsford, Ravensthorpe), T. Appleton (Rutland).

Finally thanks to all those, whether or not employed by Anglian Water, who look after the nature reserves at Anglian reservoirs and who make the reservoirs attractive to birds and to those who watch them.

A Message from the Chairman of Anglian Water

Anglian Water's reservoirs are of very great importance for wild birds and to the people who watch them. The objective of this book is to provide a readable and very useable pocket guide for the family. We hope that it will help spark a wider interest in birds, and their conservation. I am pleased that this guide has been produced with the support and endorsement of the Royal Society for the Protection of Birds.

We are very proud of the wildlife value of our reservoirs. We must never forget, however, that their primary use is for water supply and that they are of national and international significance for water sports. Achieving and maintaining a balance of uses is the key to the successful way in which such a variety of interests has been integrated. We are determined to develop still further the value of our reservoirs for bird conservation, water supply and recreation. We work closely with environmental organisations to help us achieve this.

I hope you find this book a helpful companion on your visits to our reservoirs and other waters. As a keen birdwatcher myself I know that I shall put it to good use.

Bernard Henderson, CBE
Chairman, Anglian Water.

Foreword by the Chief Executive of the Royal Society for the Protection of Birds

The Fens and marshes of the Anglian Region have all but gone, drained for agriculture. Some of the birds which frequented these lost habitats have found refuge in man-made lakes and reservoirs. The large expanses of water, shallow margins, secluded corners and adjacent grassland and scrub found on reservoirs are vital for birds at all seasons of the year.

It Is very welcome to see that Anglian Water have adopted a policy of managed access to allow people to see the wildlife on their reservoirs. Through the provision of access routes and hides on many sites, visitors are guided so they will be able to see but not disturb birds.

Several of Anglian Water's reservoirs are of outstanding national or international importance for their waterfowl populations and have been recognised as such by international designations. The wise management of them to maintain and enhance this heritage falls to Anglian Water PLC, but we all have a role to play. Through the publication of this Guide, Anglian Water is bringing to the public's attention the bird life on their reservoirs, their management and opportunities to observe them. This can only help to provide a greater understanding and appreciation of the region's importance for birds.

I would encourage everyone to use this Guide and to get to know the reservoirs and their bird life. It will lead inevitably to many hours of enjoyment and interest.

Barbara S Young
Chief Executive,
Royal Society for the Protection of Birds.

The reservoirs owned and operated by Anglian Water have gained a first class reputation for the vast numbers and the variety of species of birds which they attract and support. They offer quality birdwatching for both the beginner and experienced "birder" alike. The many nature reserves and bird hides make watching the birds, in superb surroundings, a pleasure. What could be nicer than a family outing to one of these reservoirs for a day's birdwatching!

It's not only birders who think a lot of Anglian's reservoirs. English Nature, the Government's conservation watchdog, has given four of the Company's reservoirs - Grafham Water in Cambridgeshire, Pitsford Water in Northamptonshire, Rutland Water in Leicestershire and Foxcote Reservoir in Buckinghamshire - the status of Sites of Special Scientific Interest (SSSI). In 1991 Rutland Water, Anglian's largest reservoir, was designated a Ramsar site and EC Special Protection Areas for birds. These prestigious designations give Rutland Water international importance for bird conservation.

Anglian's reservoirs are attractive to birds for many reasons. They provide a safe haven for visiting birds such as overwintering waterfowl; it is mainly for their importance for overwintering waterfowl that the reservoirs have gained their SSSI status. Migrant birds find them a congenial stopping off point on passage to and from their summer breeding grounds. Many birds stay all year. Some species of waterfowl make nests and produce young in the quieter areas around the reservoirs. Alongside the water, in grassy places and in woodland and scrub, a host of song birds forage for food and make their nests. What is really exciting to dedicated birders is the possibility of sighting a rarity. There is every chance at Anglian's reservoirs - so keep a sharp watch!

Alongside their importance for birds Anglian's reservoirs serve a vital role in the region's water supply. With the exception of the Milton Keynes lakes, which are used to control flood water, all the reservoirs described in this book were built to store water which is treated and supplied to homes, offices and factories throughout the region. The reservoirs also provide important recreation and leisure opportunities. Sailing, trout fishing and water skiing are just a few of the active pursuits available.

While water sports are very popular, most of the one million visitors a year to Anglian's reservoirs come to enjoy more leisurely pursuits. Walking or cycling in pleasant countryside provide excellent opportunities for birdwatching.

This comprehensive guide to the birds of the reservoirs will help make birdwatching easy and enjoyable. It is intended for those new to birdwatching at Anglian's reservoirs and provides a description of each of Anglian's reservoirs, where to find them and the leisure opportunities on offer. The wildlife and habitats present are clearly described together with the kinds of birds you are likely to see. Each section includes a table showing the time of year you might see each species of bird. A well-illustrated bird identification section includes detailed descriptions of more than 70 species.

Happy birdwatching!

Reservoirs are excellent places to start birdwatching. Waterfowl such as ducks, swans and grebes are for the most part large, easy to see and distinctively coloured so that their identification is not too difficult. Often several different species will be seen close together so you can make size comparisons and that, too, is a help. Until you decide to tackle the challenges of identifying more difficult species like waders, gulls and terns or - hardest of all - woodland songbirds, binoculars are not essential.

Don't take your first attempts at birdwatching too seriously. There are dedicated birders whose greatest thrill comes from grappling with the identity of some boring, nondescript brown thing lurking silently inside a dense bush. One day, if you get the bug, this may delight you too. But when you begin to look at birds it can be very disheartening that so many of them seem to look the same, or are hard to see at all. Forget about these hard ones.

The birds illustrated in this guide are all quite common and fairly easy to find. Most of them can be found at any of Anglian Water's reservoirs. Enjoy seeing them, and only when you can identify them all confidently, give thought to the many other species waiting out there to challenge, perplex and entertain you.

Using the Identification Guide

The first nine pages of the identification section deal with the waterbirds, which you are most likely to see on the reservoir itself or resting on the banks. The rest of the plates deal with other birds found at most of the sites, in woodland or scrub, on grass, running along the shoreline or hawking for insects over the water. Species which look somewhat similar are grouped on the same pages for easy comparison.

The text about each bird gives guidance on the best way to identify it, under subheadings for convenient reference.

Bird Identification

Identification summarises the main features that you should look for - sometimes shape, size or behaviour can be a better guide than the plumage markings. Birds are rarely so obliging that they stand around posing while you look in the book. Often they fly off before you can properly see, let alone memorise, details of plumage. Fortunately the vital clues are often easy to spot.

Flight

Some birds, like terns and swallows, are mostly seen in flight so you have to identify them on the wing. Many birds have quite characteristic flying styles or show distinctive patterns on their wings.

Season

When you see a bird can be an important pointer to its identity. Some species are resident here but many are migrants and present only in winter or summer. Some occur only in spring and autumn when they pass through en route between other countries.

Voice

At first, birdsongs and calls may seem impossibly difficult to learn and books are rarely much help because you cannot convey sounds properly in writing. But they are very important, especially for identifying songbirds, many of which are skilled at hiding in cover and cheeping at you - or is it jeering? Unless you. have an exceptionally retentive "ear", the best way of learning songs and calls is to concentrate on just a few each year.

Habitat, Food and Nest

Most birds have specialised ways of feeding and fixed requirements for nest sites and resting places. This means that you mostly see them in particular habitats. Differences in water depth, grass height, bush density or even the ages of trees are important. By noting the habitat in which you see a bird you can quickly rule out similar looking species with different habitat preferences.

Birdwatching at Reservoirs

It will make a lot of difference to the success of your visit - how many birds you see and how well you see them - if you go to the right areas. The reservoir descriptions in this guide tell you which areas are best for birds and how to get there.

Most reservoirs have sanctuary zones from which fishing and sailing are excluded. Waterfowl retreat into the sanctuaries when they are disturbed by recreation on the water. Thus they get some peace and quiet, and you get lots of birds concentrated where you can see them. Most of the sanctuary areas have birdwatching hides from which you can get close views of a good variety of species (and, in winter, welcome shelter from cold winds or rain).

As birds have very keen eyesight and hearing, it is vital to enter the hide and shut the door quietly. Only then, open the flaps gently and make sure you always keep your hands inside. Sometimes you will arrive and find nothing much in view. It is usually worth sitting for 10 minutes or so as birds may arrive at any moment. You are more likely to be unlucky in summer than winter when flocks of ducks are almost always present. One of the greatest values of going into a hide is that you meet other birdwatchers. Only a few of us are antisocial - most like to talk about birds and will happily tell you what is about.

Watching birds on water presents some interesting challenges. Sunlight shining towards you creates glare on the surface and birds appear as black silhouettes, especially when the sun's angle is low - at sunset or in midwinter. So select hides or viewpoints with the sun behind or to the side, depending on the time of day. Windy conditions mean that birds bob in and out of view amongst the waves. Then its easier to see them if you look from above - fortunately some reservoir carparks are perfectly sited for this. If it's cold, why not stay in the car anyway? With binoculars or a telescope you do not need to be close to the water.

In very windy weather, many ducks will seek shelter by moving to waters under the lee shore where waves are least. Look in sheltered bays and inlets. The best chance of seeing rare birds comes immediately after autumn gales in the Atlantic when powerful westerlies sometimes carry seabirds or scarce migrants inland. Easterlies from gales in the North Sea can do the same.

If you are a glutton for punishment you should also be out when it's freezing! Small waterbodies such as gravel pits freeze before the reservoirs so we can get a big influx of birds. If the cold continues, the reservoir itself will freeze but the deepest water stays open longest and it ends up crammed with all sorts of birds - practically duck soup in fact! However, there is nothing wrong with just being a fair weather birdwatcher. Birdsong and ducklings are every bit as enjoyable as Iceland gulls and Arctic skuas.

The Birdwatching Year

Each of the reservoir sections in this guide give lists of all the birds you have a reasonable chance of seeing when you visit and indicates how common or easy to see each bird is. The lists do not include scarce species or ones which may be present but are easily missed, like sparrowhawk or woodcock. With luck you may see some of them but, to compensate, you will certainly miss some of the common birds. That's birding for you!

Bird populations change with the seasons. Reservoirs have a big turnover and great variety, taken year-round. In November to February there will be large numbers of ducks, grebes and other waterfowl. Drakes are in full breeding plumage and already busy with courtship. Thousands of gulls commute in to roost in late afternoon - a splendid spectacle and noise. Wintering thrushes - fieldfare and redwing - may be present on grassy areas or stripping berries from untrimmed hedges. This is the season for thermal underwear; reservoirs can be bitterly cold places as you peer, eyes streaming, into the teeth of a northeaster, searching for that elusive smew.

During March and April wintering wildfowl depart and those which remain split up into breeding pairs. The first mallard duckling broods appear. Sand martins are amongst the earliest summer visitors, some arriving in March, but most migrants appear in April especially after a few days with warm southerly winds. Birdsong variety and volume increase daily and this is a good season to look for the smaller songbirds such as finches, buntings and warblers as they are easier to see now than when everything is in full leaf and they are busy incubating eggs and rearing young.

In May and June most migration is complete though some waders which breed in the high Arctic are still passing through here in May, delaying their departure until their nesting grounds have thawed out. Swifts are one of the last of our visitors to arrive and will depart again in August. But for most birds this is the height of the breeding season and song tails off in June as adults busy themselves with feeding ever-hungry young.

From July to October is another period of movement and change. The first of the southward-bound migrant waders can appear in July but most waders pass through in August and September. Reservoir draw-down is usually well advanced by now and this attracts them by exposing muddy margins where they can refuel. Our own summer visitors begin to leave in August, most depart in September and a few linger until October by which time the winter visitors are streaming in.

Taking the year as a whole, August is often the dullest month but by contrast September usually offers the biggest variety of birds and, frequently, good weather to enjoy them. However, many are in worn, dowdy plumage or are rather nondescript juveniles so that month also brings its share of identification problems.

Binoculars, Telescopes and Bird Photography

If you become seriously interested in birds, you will want to buy binoculars. Take time to choose with care. Optical quality and robustness are important. Broadly, you get what you pay for. It is by far the best to go to a specialist dealer (see adverts in the RSPB magazine BIRDS or one of the birdwatching monthlies). Try out several pairs. Best of all, go to the annual birdwatching fair at Rutland Water and test pairs in the field before buying.

Binoculars are described as "8 x 40" or "10 x 50", for example. The first figure is the magnification and the second is the diameter (in mm) of each object lens, through which light enters the binoculars. Dividing the latter by the former gives the "light value". Thus the light value of a pair of 8 x 40s is 5. The higher the value the brighter the image you will see. However the quality of the lenses and prisms themselves also affects light throughout. With good binoculars a light value of 4 is acceptable. With "cheapos" 5 is a safer bet. This matters a lot because you will be birding at times in poor light - overcast, raining or at dusk.

You need a magnification of 8 or 10 - less gives too small an image, more exaggerates shake and tends to blur the image. Larger magnifications and bigger object lenses also mean more weight. Binoculars can be tiring to wear and near-impossible to use if they are too heavy. Pick what you are sure you will be comfortable with. Macho-man 15 x 60s are only suitable for U-boat commanders.

Do not hurry to buy a telescope. They are invaluable for big waters like Grafham, but also cumbersome and require practice to use well. Follow the same rules that apply to binoculars - above all remember that good light transmission is more important than high power. Try out your friends' scopes before you buy. But beware; some birders are more fashion-conscious than they will admit and this year's new £600 model which has everyone in ecstasies may be only marginally better than some less trendy stalwart which has been around for years and costs less than half. Finally, do not skimp on the tripod. A telescope on a weedy stand wobbles about uselessly in the slightest breeze.

Many reservoirs offer good opportunities to photograph birds. Hides can put you close to birds resting, feeding, in courtship or territorial conflict. Many people get excellent results with a 400 mm lens hand held. Perhaps the biggest secret of success is not to try both to watch birds and to photograph them - you end up so cluttered with optics that you can scarcely walk. Bird photography is best done on your own, from an empty hide and without time constraints. You cannot hurry good pictures.

Field Notes and Records

Field notes help you to identify, learn and memorise the key features of birds. Learn to draw simple two-oval bird shapes. These provide a basis on which to mark distinctive features and proportions such as length of beak, legs and tail. There are standard names for different plumage areas on a bird's body. You will find these set out in most field guides to bird identification. Frankly, though they probably should, most birdwatchers never get round to learning all of these. At least to begin with, concentrate on recording obvious and distinctive plumage patterns, paying particular attention to eyestripes and face markings as these are often very helpful in separating otherwise similar species. With flying birds, look for wing-patterns, for the same reason.

When you see a rare species, you ought to submit a record of it to the county bird recorder. Your record will have no chance of being accepted unless you can produce a description made at the time you saw the bird.

Whether or not you make field notes, you will almost certainly make lists of birds seen on each trip. These do help you develop a feel for what birds you can expect to see at different seasons and that helps enormously with identification by narrowing the field of choice.

From your trip lists, you can compile an annual list and, of course, a life list. Really keen, or possibly deranged, birders have special lists such as "birds seen from trains" and "birds seen on TV". "Birds seen while lying in bed" has a lot going for it.

Birdwatching Clubs

One of the best and most pleasant ways of learning about birds is to join the county bird club or natural history society, or the RSPB's local members' group. They run year-round field trips and usually have a winter programme of indoor meetings and talks.

Caring for Birds

The welfare of the bird always comes first. Our aims should always be not to disturb birds and not to damage their habitats. Special care is needed when birds are nesting. If you are watching a bird which is obviously agitated or distressed, you are probably keeping it away from its nest, so move on.

Remember too that in extreme cold you put birds' lives at risk if you disturb them and make them use up vital reserves of energy which they may be unable to replenish until the thaw comes.

All birds, their nests and eggs are protected by law and if you see an offence committed you should report it to the police or the RSPB. The law makes provision for a small number of species which can cause damage to be shot by authorised people - the birds involved include crows and woodpigeons. In addition, the commoner species of wildfowl can be shot during the winter months. Anglian Water does not permit wildfowling to take place on its land.

Wildfowl Counts, Bird Ringing and Conservation Activities

The numbers of wildfowl wintering on Anglian Water reservoirs are so large that they are of international importance for conservation. The totals are checked monthly as part of a national counting programme which covers all the bigger waterbodies in the UK. Help with counts is always welcome and you can contact the local organiser through the Wildfowl and Wetlands Trust (see Useful Addresses).

Wildfowl are just one group of birds which undertake major long-distance migrations. In order to learn about the migration movements of birds, their lifespans and the causes of mortality, many nations run ringing programmes. Rings are put on nestlings or on adults which are caught in special nets. In the UK, ringers must be trained and licensed. The British Trust for Ornithology runs the ringing programme. Each bird ring carries a unique number and an address for its return. If you find a dead bird, perhaps washed-up on the shoreline, check its legs for a ring. If it has one, prise it off and mail it to the address stamped on it, saying when and where you found it. In return you will receive a note telling you where and when the bird was originally ringed - perhaps nearby but possibly as far off as Greenland or Siberia.

The practical application of research, in terms of active conservation programmes on the ground, brings us to the work of the RSPB and the County Wildlife Trusts. The RSPB's work is nationwide and, indeed, international. In the Anglian Water area there are plenty of RSPB members' groups which have a wide range of activities to support its objectives.

If you want to give practical help to reserve management, contact the relevant County Wildlife Trust. There are Trust reserves at many of the reservoirs where assistance is likely to be warmly welcomed.

Anglian Water Reservoirs

CADNEY

Grimsby

COVENHAM

Lincoln

COSTESSEY PITS

Norwich

Stamford

Peterborough

RUTLAND WATER

Corby

HOLLOWELL

RAVENSTHORPE

PITSFORD

GRAFHAM WATER

Northampton

Bury St. Edmunds

WILLEN LAKE

Cambridge

Ipswich

Bedford

ALTON WATER

FOXCOTE

CALDECOTTE

HYDE LANE

Milton Keynes

ARDLEIGH

Colchester

Chelmsford

The Anglian Water Region is the largest of the 10 regional water companies of England and Wales. Its 27,000 square kilometres stretch from the Humber to the Thames.

This vast region encompasses a rich variety of landscapes including the Country's only wetland national park - the Norfolk and Suffolk Broads. The flat lands of the fens and the characteristic heaths and pines of Breckland contrast with the undulating countryside of the Lincolnshire Wolds, the internationally important estuaries of Essex and the Wash and the beautiful coast of North Norfolk. Anglian's reservoirs add to this richness. To the west of the region some of the larger reservoirs have become major tourist attractions as well as being an important source of water to Anglian's customers.

Rutland Water in Leicestershire is Anglian's largest reservoir. It is situated in pleasant rolling countryside and offers a superb range of leisure activities. Rutland is of the very highest value for birds. Its nature reserve is run in partnership with the Leicestershire and Rutland Trust for Nature Conservation and each year hosts the British Birdwatching Fair.

At the other end of the scale are smaller waters such as those at Costessey Pits. The woodland and water at Costessey Pits provide an important local amenity on the outskirts of Norwich. Together with water skiing and good fishing they provide an attractive range of habitats for birds in this picturesque part of the Wensum valley.

Between the small and the large come the 12 other waters described in this book. Nearly all of these are easily accessible and open to visitors. They include Grafham Water in Cambridgeshire which is a Site of Special Scientific Interest (SSSI) and hosts international sailing events. Pitsford Water is also a SSSI and is set in attractive Northamptonshire countryside. Rutland Water, Grafham Water and Pitsford are all used for water supply and are known collectively as the Ruthamford group of reservoirs. Each is situated in the west of the Anglian region and provides excellent trout fishing.

By way of complete contrast Alton Water is to be found in south-east Suffolk and is a first class coarse fishery. Alton is Suffolk's largest body of freshwater and is an excellent place to watch birds. It is particularly good for birdwatching in hard winters when neighbouring areas of freshwater have frozen over.

Alongside reservoirs used for water supply, Anglian controls balancing reservoirs which are used to control flows of water to prevent flooding at times of heavy rain. The most significant of these are in Milton Keynes where the balancing reservoirs have been integrated into the development of this new city to form important local amenities providing a wide range of leisure opportunities. They have become of great importance for birds and, being at the heart of the city, are, not surprisingly, well watched!

Whether in urban or rural areas Anglian Water reservoirs make a positive contribution to nature conservation and the landscape, and provide first class leisure opportunities.

In the sections that follow each reservoir is described. Information is provided on where to find them and what water sports and other leisure opportunities are on offer. The birds and other wildlife and where to see them are described. A birdwatching calendar is also included for each reservoir so that you will know what kinds of bird you might expect to see at any time of the year. This lists birds by families which is the conventional method used in bird books. Note that in the identification section of this Guide some birds are arranged in a slightly different sequence so as to group those that look similar, even if they are not related because this may help you to identify them.

Key to Reservoir Site Plans

KEY:			
Cafe	🗋	Parking	Ⓟ
Hide	H	Picnic Area	⋒
Information	*i*	Toilets	T
Nature Reserve	NR	Woodland	◻

Alton Water

Alton Water lies in Tattingstone Valley, a most picturesque part of the Suffolk countryside to the south of Ipswich, between Tattingstone and Holbrook.

Winding back up a long valley, with creeks and backwaters tucked away on both banks, Alton Water is most attractive. Woods, rolling arable fields and grassland surround it, while to the south the skyline is dominated by the handsome facade of the Royal Hospital School with its impressive tower.

Alton Water

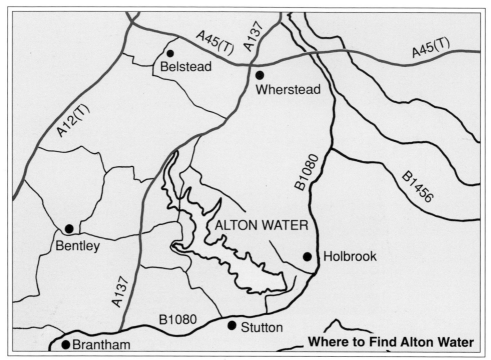

Where to Find Alton Water

Alton Water near Ipswich can be easily reached from the south and the west along the A12 and A45. Join the A137 at Wherstead and then the B1080 to Stutton. Just after Stutton you will see the reservoir signposted. When you get there parking your car isn't a problem as there are several car parks dotted around the reservoir, the one in the visitor centre having toilets.

The reservoir provides the main source of water for Ipswich and the southern part of Suffolk but has also been developed for the benefit of wildlife and enjoyment of the public.

The valley was formerly a mixed area of scrub, woodland, rough grazing, pasture and arable land with Holbrook Mill Stream running through it. When the 168 hectare reservoir was constructed, in the 1970's, particular effort was made to preserve features such as Alton Hall Mill. The Mill was carefully dismantled brick by brick and re-erected at the Museum of Rural Life in Stowmarket, where you can see it grinding corn once again. Important wildlife habitats such as areas of woodland,

totalling 9 hectares, have also been retained and are now carefully managed. Furthermore, some 40,000 oak, beech, birch and chestnut have also been planted to provide additional woodland for you to enjoy in the years to come.

Overlooking the reservoir on the south-west shore is Tattingstone Place, which dates back to Edward the Confessor. In 1761 the invalid owner, Sir Roger White, built the nearby Tattingstone Wonder, a church style building, originally comprising workers' cottages and since converted to a single home. Tattingstone Wonder overlooks one of the designated nature reserves. This area of shallow water has been managed for wildlife. The Suffolk Wildlife Trust has set up a conservation group to record breeding and migrant birds, butterflies, mammals, plants and other wildlife. If you would like to help collect information on the wildlife around Alton Water please pick up a record card at the Alton Water visitor centre (opposite the main car park). Casual sightings and observations are equally as important as results from organised surveys. If you wish to help with the collation of

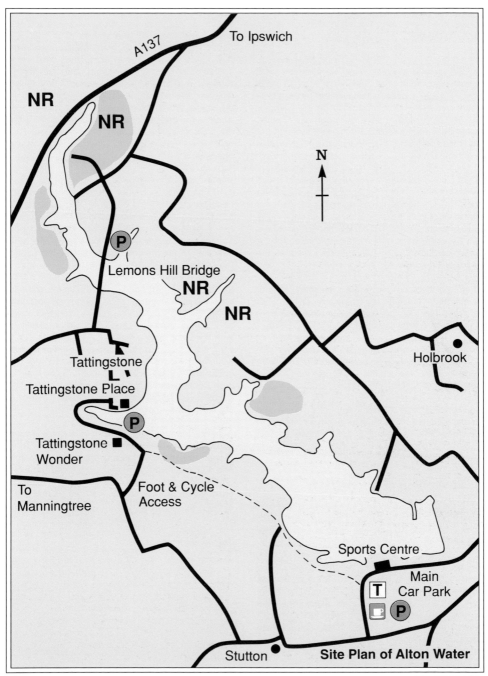

To Ipswich

A137

NR

NR

N

P

Lemons Hill Bridge

NR

NR

Tattingstone

Tattingstone Place

Tattingstone Wonder

P

To Manningtree

Foot & Cycle Access

Holbrook

Sports Centre

Main Car Park

T

P

Stutton

Site Plan of Alton Water

Key, see page 14

information about the reservoir's wildlife please contact the Trust using the address given at the back of this book.

If you feel energetic there is an 12.8 kilometre footpath around the reservoir. This attractive walk is well signposted. For those who want to relax why not have a picnic at one of the picnic areas where you can watch the activity on the water or just sit back and admire the scenery. Please remember to keep to the waymarked footpaths in the Nature Reserves to keep disturbance to wildlife to a minimum.

What else is on offer? Well, the reservoir, which holds 9,080,000 cubic metres and has a maximum depth of 18 metres, provides some of the best coarse angling in the area. Species present include Carp, Tench, Roach, Rudd, Perch, Bream, Pike and Eels. Permits can be obtained from a number of fishing tackle outlets in the area and at the visitor centre.

Other recreational activities include sailing, windsurfing, rowing and subaqua diving. For details of hiring facilities and rates please enquire at the Water Sports Centre or ring (0473) 328408.

The new visitor centre has been built together with a surfaced cycle track around part of the reservoir. Cycle hire will be available. Other new facilities will include a play area for children and catering.

If you would like further information about the reservoir, its leisure facilities or points of interest in the immediate surrounding area please contact Anglian's Customer Relations Staff on Colchester (0206) 774000.

Birdwatching at Alton Water

For birdwatchers, the site has several attractions. First, it offers a good variety of habitats, each with its characteristic assemblage of birds - deepwater and shallows, open shores and well-reeded inlets, some old timber and plenty of newer plantations, well-grown scrub, hedges, rough grassland and short-mown amenity areas. Second, the water area is narrow so that even birds on the opposite banks are often less than 500 metres away, while the sloping banks give you that extra bit of height which makes viewing easier. Third, that intricate shoreline tempts you onward because you don't know what may be hiding in the next inlet.

The circular footpath route makes it possible to spend all day ambling around Alton Water if you wish. Alternatively, in the course of a couple of hours, you can briskly view the southern end from the banks near the main car parks, drive up to Tattingstone Wonder to check out the middle reaches and finally park at Lemon's Bay to see what's in the nature reserve by walking north along the shore. While you're here, it's also a good idea to cross the bridge and work your way south along the western bank. This puts the sun at your back and gives you excellent views into the creeks opposite.

Winter wildfowl numbers typically reach about 1,400 birds in December and January. This total usually includes about 600 coot, 300 mallard, 300 tufted duck and 100-150 pochard. There are also fair numbers of great crested grebe, wigeon, greylag and Canada geese, plus a sprinkle of other species. The north end of the reservoir is usually the best area for the diving ducks.

In spring, the grasslands near the main car park attract yellow wagtail and, sometimes passage wheatear. Nightingales sing from Crag Hall Wood and Larch Wood. These and other areas of woodland and scrub may have a good variety of warblers in summer - blackcap and garden warbler, whitethroat, lesser whitethroat, willow warbler and chiffchaff. Around adjoining arable fields look for corn bunting and listen for its jangling song. This species is becoming very localised due to changing farming practice.

Autumn brings a good variety of migrant waders especially if the waterlevel is drawn down. Incidentally, in winter there is often a roost of gulls and waders including ringed plover and turnstone on the ploughed field to the east of the main car park: these birds commute from the nearby coast at high tide.

For up-to-minute information on "what's about" drop in at the visitor centre.

Alton Water Birdwatching Calendar

Species	Mar-April	May-June	July-Oct	Nov-Feb
Great Crested Grebe	••••	••••	••••	••••
Little Grebe	•			•
Cormorant	••••	••	•••	••••
Grey Heron	••	•	••	••
Mallard	••••	••••	••••	••••
Teal	•••		•••	••••
Gadwall	•••	•	•	••••
Wigeon				••
Pintail				•
Shoveler	••	•	•	•
Tufted Duck	•••	•	•••	••••
Pochard	•••		•	••••
Goldeneye	•			••
Shelduck	•			•
Greylag Goose	••••	••••	••••	••••
Canada Goose	••••	•••	•••	••••
Mute Swan	•••	•••	•••	•••
Sparrowhawk	•	•	•	•
Kestrel	•••	•••	•••	•••
Red-legged Partridge	•	•	•	•
Pheasant	••	••	••	••
Moorhen	••••	••••	••••	••••
Coot	••••	••••	••••	••••
Oystercatcher				•
Lapwing	••••	•••	•••	••••
Ringed Plover	•	•	•	••
Snipe	••	•	•	••
Green Sandpiper	•	•	••	•
Common Sandpiper		•	••	
Redshank				•
Greenshank			•	
Little Stint			•	
Dunlin				•
Curlew Sandpiper			•	
Ruff			•	
Gt Black-backed Gull				•
Lesser "	•		•	•
Herring Gull				•
Common Gull	••••		••••	••••
Black-headed Gull	••••	••••	••••	••••
Black Tern		•		
Common Tern	•••	•••	•••	
Stock Dove	••	••	••	••
Woodpigeon	••••	••••	••••	••••
Turtle Dove		••	••	
Cuckoo	•	•		
Tawny Owl	•	•	•	•
Swift		•••	•••	
Green Woodpecker	•	•	•	•
Gt Spotted Woodpecker	••	••	••	••
Skylark	•••	•••	•••	•••
Swallow	•••	••••	••••	
House Martin		••••	••••	
Sand Martin	•••	••••	••••	
Carrion Crow	•••	•••	•••	•••
Rook	•••	•••	•••	•••
Jackdaw	•			•
Magpie	••	••	••	••
Great Tit	••••	••••	••••	••••
Blue Tit	••••	••••	••••	••••
Long-tailed Tit	•	•	•	•
Nuthatch	•	•	•	•
Treecreeper	•	•	•	•
Wren	••••	••••	••••	••••
Mistle Thrush	••	••	••	••
Fieldfare				•
Song Thrush	•••	•••	•••	•••
Redwing				•••
Blackbird	••••	••••	••••	••••
Winchat			•	
Wheatear	•		•	
Nightingale		•	•	
Robin	••••	••••	••••	••••
Reed Warbler			•	
Sedge Warbler			••	••
Blackcap	••		••	••
Garden Warbler			••	••
Whitethroat			•••	•••
Lesser Whitethroat			•	•
Willow Warbler	•••	•••	•••	
Chiffchaff	••		••	••
Goldcrest	•	•	•	•
Spotted Flycatcher		•	•	
Dunnock	••••	••••	••••	••••
Meadow Pipit	•••	•••	•••	••
Pied Wagtail	••	••	••	••
Yellow Wagtail	••••	••••	••••	
Starling	••••	••••	••••	••••
Greenfinch	•••	•••	•••	•••
Goldfinch	•••	•••	•••	•••
Linnet	•••	••	••	•••
Redpoll	•			
Bullfinch	••	••	••	••
Chaffinch	•••	•••	•••	•••
Corn Bunting	•	•	•	•
Yellowhammer	••	••	••	••
Reed Bunting	••	••	••	••
House Sparrow	••••	••••	••••	••••

Recent rarities include:- Purple Heron, Quail, Roseate Tern, Pied Flycatcher, Red-backed Shrike.

Key: •••• Normally present/more than 90% of time
••• Frequently present/50%-90% of time
•• Less common/10-50% of time
• Scarce/less than 10% of time but not a rarity

Ardleigh Reservoir

Ardleigh Reservoir nestles in a picturesque valley amid beautiful Constable country. It is hard to believe this secluded spot is less than a 2 minute drive from the busy A12 and about 3 kilometres from the centre of Colchester.

The reservoir was formed by constructing an earth dam across two tributaries of Salary Brook which explains its V-shape. Covering 57 hectares the reservoir holds 2,200,000 cubic metres and is fed from the River Colne.

Ardleigh was opened in 1971 to meet the demand of the expanding populations of Colchester and Tendring Peninsular, and currently produces approximately 24,600 cubic metres per day when used together with existing underground sources. Besides its primary water supply function the reservoir also supports two major sports facilities - sailing and fishing.

Ardleigh Reservoir

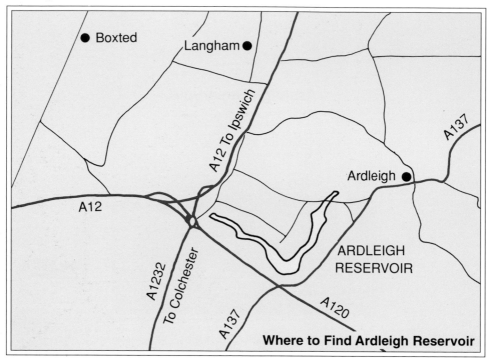

Boxted

Langham

A12 To Ipswich

A137

A12

Ardleigh

A1232

To Colchester

A137

ARDLEIGH RESERVOIR

A120

Where to Find Ardleigh Reservoir

Ardleigh Reservoir, near Colchester, can be easily reached from the A12. From Colchester itself take the A1232 north for about 3 kilometres. You will find free car parking is available just off Crown Lane on the north shore and by the fishing lodge near the dam to the south. The latter has toilets.

The reservoir is managed by the Ardleigh Reservoir Committee composed of representatives of Anglian Water and Tendring Hundred Water Company.

Ardleigh Sailing Club operates from a club house on the south shore near the dam and sailing is open to members only. However, membership is reasonable and this thriving club organises club and open events for various types of craft as well as offering sailing courses with expert tuition. For more details contact: Ardleigh Sailing Club, c/o Ardleigh Reservoir, Clover Way, Ardleigh, Colchester, Essex CO7 7PT

Fishermen will probably be aware that Ardleigh has rapidly become established as one of the country's foremost trout fisheries since its opening in 1971. In the early 1980's it was also opened as a coarse fishery, following the trout season, and was soon recognised nationally as one of the top roach fisheries.

Fishing is allowed from 8.00 am until dusk and permits can be obtained from the new Fishing Lodge near the dam on the south shore. The office opens at 7.30 am. You can buy Ardleigh tied flies here and hire tackle or a boat. The fishery runs a fleet of twenty seven fishing boats, one being specially adapted for disabled fishermen. If you want to brush up your skills, there are courses available which cater for improvers as well as beginners. Alternatively you can book private lessons.

For advance bookings, applications for tuition or general enquiries, drop in to the Fishing Lodge where the staff will be pleased to help, or contact: The Fisheries & Estates Officer, Ardleigh Reservoir, Clover Way, Ardleigh, Colchester CO7 7PT Tel: (0206) 230642.

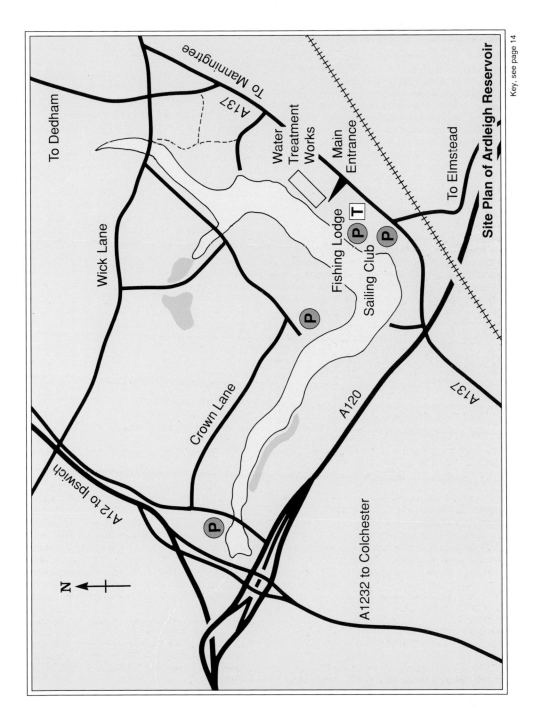

Site Plan of Ardleigh Reservoir

Key, see page 14

Birdwatching at Ardleigh Reservoir

A very pleasant and secluded site, Ardleigh Reservoir is at its best in summer when the trees and scrub which fringe its banks hold a wide variety of songbirds – warblers and finches, titmice, turtle doves and thrushes. As the season progresses, there are usually broods of young great crested grebes, moorhens and coots, mallard ducklings and mute swan cygnets.

In spring and autumn the open, mown grassland by the dam may attract passage migrants including wheatear, pipits and wagtails. Winter wildfowl numbers are not large, but it is always worth looking for birds sheltering on the three lagoons which are separated from the main body of the reservoir by the lanes around its northern sites.

The whole of the north shores are accessible from Wide Lane and Crown Lane, where there are several entry points with stiles or off-road parking on the wide grass verges. Best of all, the fisherman's carpark opposite the dam gives access to an attractive, firm-surfaced path right along the length of the north western side. Birders in a hurry can "do" the whole site in about an hour but where's the pleasure in that? On a fine day you can spend several enjoyable hours pottering or picnicking around the water.

Please note birdwatching is by permit only but these can easily be obtained by ringing (0206) 230685 preferably the day before.

Ardleigh Birdwatching Calendar

Species	Mar-April	May-June	July-Oct	Nov-Feb
Gt Crested Grebe	••••	••••	••••	••••
Little Grebe	••	•••	•••	••
Cormorant	••••	••••	••••	••••
Grey Heron	••••	••••	••••	••••
Mallard	••••	••••	••••	••••
Teal	•••		•••	••••
Gadwall	•••	•	•	••••
Wigeon				••
Shoveler	•			•
Tufted Duck	••••	••••	••••	••••
Pochard	••••		•	••••
Goldeneye	•			•
Greylag Goose	••••	••••	••••	••••
Canada Goose	••••	••••	••••	••••
Mute Swan	••••	••••	••••	••••
Sparrowhawk	•	•	•	•
Kestrel	••	••	••	••
Pheasant	•	•	•	•
Moorhen	••••	••••	••••	••••
Coot	••••	••••	••••	••••
Oystercatcher				•
Lapwing	••••	•••	•••	••••
Ringed Plover	•		•	•
Snipe	•		•	•
Green Sandpiper	•		•	
Common Sandpiper		•	••	
Redshank			•	•
Greenshank			•	
Dunlin				•
Gt Black-backed Gull				•
Lesser "	•		•	•
Herring Gull	•		•	•
Common Gull	••••		••••	••••
Black-headed Gull	••••	••••	••••	••••
Black Tern		•		
Common Tern	•••	•••	•••	
Stock Dove	•••	•••	•••	•••
Woodpigeon	••••	••••	••••	••••
Turtle Dove		•••	•••	
Collard Dove	••	••	••	••
Cuckoo	•	•••	•	
Swift		••••	••••	
Gt Spotted Woodpecker	•	•	•	•
Skylark	••	••	••	••
Swallow	•••	••••	••••	
House Martin	•••	••••	••••	
Sand Martin	•••	••••	••••	
Carrion Crow	••••	••••	••••	••••
Rook	•••	•••	•••	•••
Jackdaw	••	••	••	••
Magpie	••••	••••	••••	••••
Great Tit	••••	••••	••••	••••
Blue Tit	••••	••••	••••	••••
Coal Tit	•	•	•	•
Willow Tit	•	•	•	•
Long-tailed Tit	•••	•••	•••	•••

Species	Mar-April	May-June	July-Oct	Nov-Feb
Treecreeper	•	•	•	•
Wren	••••	••••	••••	••••
Mistle Thrush	••••	••••	••••	••••
Fieldfare				•
Song Thrush	••••	••••	••••	••••
Redwing				•
Blackbird	••••	••••	••••	••••
Wheatear	•		•	
Robin	••••	••••	••••	••••
Reed Warbler	•••	••••	•••	
Sedge Warbler	•••	••••	••••	
Blackcap	•••	•••	•••	
Garden Warbler	•••	•••	•••	
Whitethroat	•••	••••	•••	
Lesser Whitethroat	••	•••	••	
Willow Warbler	•••	••••	••••	
Chiffchaff	•••	••••	•••	
Goldcrest	••	••	••	••
Spotted Flycatcher	••	•••	•••	
Dunnock	••••	••••	••••	••••
Meadow Pipit	•••		•••	•••
Pied Wagtail	••••	••••	••••	••••
Yellow Wagtail	••	•	••	
Starling	••••	••••	••••	••••
Greenfinch	•••	•••	•••	•••
Goldfinch	•••	••••	••••	•••
Linnet	•••	•••	•••	•••
Redpoll	•••	•••	•••	•••
Bullfinch	••	••	••	••
Chaffinch	••••	••••	••••	••••
Yellowhammer	•••	•••	•••	•••
Reed Bunting	••••	••••	••••	••••
House Sparrow	••••	••••	••••	••••

Key: •••• Normally present/more than 90% of time
••• Frequently present/50%-90% of time
•• Less common/10-50% of time
• Scarce/less than 10% of time but not a rarity

Cadney Reservoir

Cadney reservoir is the most northerly of Anglian's reservoirs and one of the smallest and is situated in a flat area of countryside.

The lack of a natural valley which could be dammed meant that it had to be built by forming embankments. These contain the water and make the reservoir a fairly regular rectangular shape when viewed from above.

Cadney Reservoir

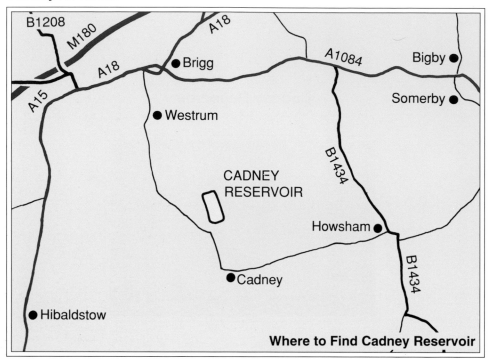

Where to Find Cadney Reservoir

Cadney reservoir is situated near Brigg in Humberside, just off the M180, and can be approached via the road to Cadney village from Brigg or from the B1434. The reservoir is just to the north of Cadney village.

Cadney was opened in 1974. It can hold about 900,000 cubic metres of water and has a surface area of approximately 14 hectares. Water is pumped into the reservoir from the River Ancholme which flows nearby. Water from the reservoir is treated at Elsham water treatment works before being used to supply customers in South Humberside.

For reasons of safety casual public access is not available, Cadney is about 11 metres deep and has very steeply sloping sides. Permission to watch the birds at Cadney can, however, be obtained by telephoning Anglian Water Customer Relations staff on (0522) 557000. There are a number of people who regularly watch and record the birds by special arrangement.

Despite its small size Cadney offers opportunities for water skiing, sailing and diving through the Cadney Carrs Water Sports Association.

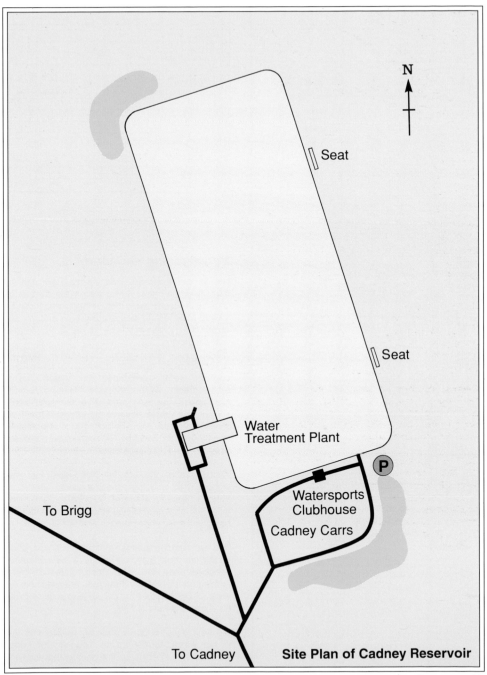

N

Seat

Seat

Water
Treatment Plant

P

Watersports
Clubhouse

Cadney Carrs

To Brigg

To Cadney

Site Plan of Cadney Reservoir

Key, see page 14

Cadney Birdwatching Calendar

Species	Mar-April	May-June	July-Oct	Nov-Feb
Great Crested Grebe	••••	•••	•••	••••
Red-necked Grebe				•
Little Grebe				••
Cormorant	••••	•••	•••	••••
Grey Heron	••••	•••	•••	••••
Mallard	••••	•••	•••	••••
Teal				•••
Gadwall				•
Wigeon				•
Tufted Duck	••••			••••
Pochard	••			••••
Goosander				••
Shelduck				•••
Greylag Goose				••
Canada Goose	•••			••
Sparrowhawk	••	••	••	••
Kestrel	••••	••••	••••	••••
Red-legged Partridge	••••	••••	••••	••••
Partridge	••••	••••	••••	••••
Pheasant	••••	••••	••••	••••
Coot				••
Oystercatcher			•	•
Lapwing	•	•••	•••	•
Ringed Plover			•••	
Little Ringed Plover			•••	
Golden Plover			••	
Snipe			••	
Woodcock				••
Redshank	•••			•••
Greenshank			•	
Gt Black-backed Gull	••			••
Lesser "	••			••
Herring Gull	••			••
Common Gull	•••			••••
Black-headed Gull	••••	•••	•••	••••
Common Tern			••	
Stock Dove	••••	••••	••••	••••
Woodpigeon	••••	••••	••••	••••
Turtle Dove		••		
Collard Dove	••	••	••	••
Cuckoo		••		
Barn Owl	•	•	•	•
Little Owl	•	•	•	•
Swift		•••		
Skylark	••••	••••	••••	
Swallow	••	••••	••••	
House Martin	••	••••	••••	
Sand Martin	•			
Carrion Crow	•••	•••	•••	•••
Rook	••••	••••	••••	••••
Magpie	•••	•••	•••	•••
Great Tit	••	••	••	••
Blue Tit	••	••	••	••
Mistle Thrush	••	••	••	••
Fieldfare				•••
Song Thrush	••	••	••	••
Redwing				•••
Blackbird	••••	••••	••••	••••
Wheatear	•			
Robin	••	••	••	••
Sedge Warbler		•		
Whitethroat	•			
Pied Wagtail	•••	•••	•••	•••
Grey Wagtail	•••	•••	•••	•••
Starling	••••	••••	••••	••••
Greenfinch	•••			•••
Goldfinch	•			•
Linnet	•••	•••	•••	•••
Bullfinch	•	•	•	•
Chaffinch	•••	•••	•••	•••
Yellowhammer	••	•••	•••	
House Sparrow	•••	•••	•••	•••

Recent rarities include:- Shag

Key: •••• Normally present/more than 90% of time
••• Frequently present/50%-90% of time
•• Less common/10-50% of time
• Scarce/less than 10% of time but not a rarity

Birdwatching at Cadney

Not to mince words, Cadney reservoir can be forbidding and bleak. Fortunately, birds don't judge sites by the same rules that we apply and it can be a worthwhile site to visit especially in autumn and winter. It is, however, likely to be a two-thermal vest excursion.

A large raised reservoir, Cadney is basically a concrete tank surrounded by steep, grassy embankments so that the water level is perched high above the flat, productive farmland which surrounds it and is accordingly exposed to all the winds of heaven. Anything from 100 to 400 wildfowl can be present in winter, with red-necked grebe a scarce but not rare occurence.

Though conditions are far from ideal for most waders, half a dozen species usually occur on autumn passage. Perhaps surprisingly, grey wagtail is not infrequent at any time of the year, despite being generally uncommon in eastern England.

The surrounding grassy embankment and small plantations hold a typical range of the commoner songbirds and are sometimes quartered by a hunting barn owl. Grey partridges are regular in the area; once abundant in the Anglian region, these birds are now hard to find.

It is best to visit on days when the watersports club is not active. Ideally go on Thursday or Friday when birds disturbed on the preceeding weekend are likely to have returned.

Caldecotte Lake

Caldecotte Lake in Milton Keynes is a 44 hectare lake constructed in the 1980's to help alleviate local flooding problems. It is designed to hold, temporarily, 700,000 cubic metres of rainwater which pours off rooftops and roads into drains and the river. After heavy rain, water from the River Ouzel, which flows through Milton Keynes, can be diverted into the lake via the computer controlled weir gates. It is held there until the swollen river subsides and the excess water can be discharged back into it gradually, so preventing flooding downstream.

Caldecotte provides an informal leisure area where you can get away from the bustle of city life and unwind in the surrounding parkland which has been extensively planted with trees and shrubs.

Caldecotte Lake

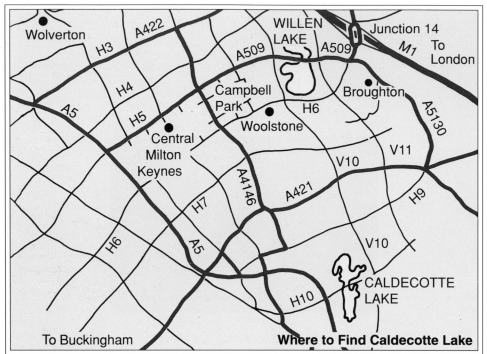

Where to Find Caldecotte Lake

Caldecotte Lake is only ten minutes drive from Milton Keynes city centre. The lake has two basins bisected by Bletcham Way (H10).

It can easily be reached from the A5, with parking just off Bletcham Way, or by leaving the M1 motorway at J14 and taking the A5130. You then follow the A421 Groveway (H9) until you turn left onto Brickhill Street (V10). Turning right from this down Chase Avenue, through the Walton Park Estate, you will quickly reach the lakeside and should have no difficulty in parking. There are two car parks on Simpson Road, (off Chase Avenue) one of which has a pleasant picnic area.

Caldecotte Lake is a pleasant place to have a picnic or just sit and relax. The leisure trail offers a surfaced path for you to walk or jog round the lake.

Wheelchair users should have little difficulty exploring or enjoying a spot of birdwatching.

A bridleway passes along the north basin and for the energetic explorer you can pick up the 'Red Way' cycle route, an extensive system of cycleways through Milton Keynes. Just follow the signs.

Water sports are run by a consortium of private clubs and a youth activity centre on the lake.

For further information contact Milton Keynes Parks, 26 Erica Road, Stacey Bushes, Milton Keynes, MK12 6LD tel (0908) 223322. Or take the short drive to the excellent Watersports Centre on Willen Lake where you can try windsurfing, sailing or canoeing.

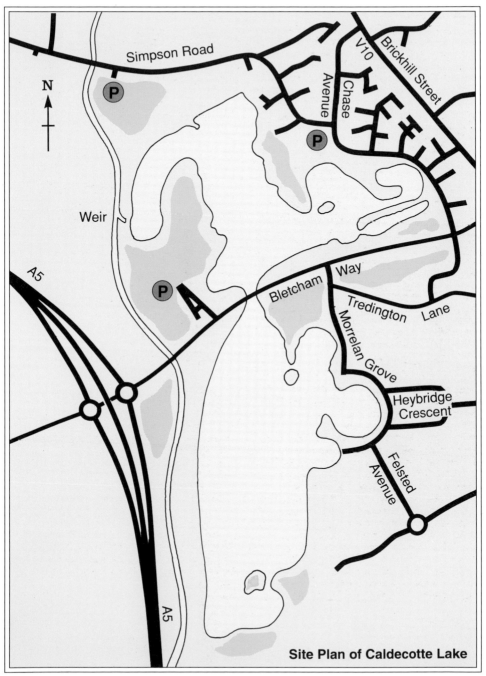

Site Plan of Caldecotte Lake

N

Simpson Road

P

Weir

P

A

Avenue

Chase

V10

Brickhill Street

P

Bletcham   Way

Tredington   Lane

Morrelan Grove

Heybridge Crescent

Felsted Avenue

A5

A5

Key, see page 14

33

Birdwatching at Caldecotte

Though it attracts rather smaller numbers of waterfowl than Willen Lake – the maximum rarely rises above 600 birds – the range of species is similar, with greylag and Canada geese, wigeon, mallard, tufted duck, pochard and coot most numerous. The variety of waders recorded on migration is fairly small. On the other hand, the surrounding land attracts several species not found at Willen, such as lesser spotted woodpecker, willow tit and treecreeper. You are also more likely to see green and great spotted woodpeckers here.

Like many other reservoirs, the lake is surrounded by large areas of grass. Depending on how it is managed, grass can be a notably good bird habitat. In fact birds themselves can affect its value – geese and wigeon create a short sward useful to foraging mistle thrush, fieldfare and redwing, wheatears and pied and yellow wagtail.

Older grassland with ants' nests attracts green woodpecker which use their long, barbed tongues – evolved for harpooning wood-boring insects – to feed on ant larvae & pupae. Rougher grass which is allowed to seed is favoured by yellowhammers and, because it harbours small mammals, attracts hunting owls and kestrels.

Access is easy from the V10 and the H10 and there are good paths.

Caldecotte Lake Birdwatching Calendar

Species	Mar-April	May-June	July-Oct	Nov-Feb
Gt. Crested Grebe	••••	••••	••••	••••
Little Grebe	•••	•••	••••	••••
Cormorant	••	•	•••	••••
Grey Heron	••••	•••	••••	••••
Mallard	••••	••••	••••	••••
Teal	••••	•	••••	••••
Gadwall	••••	•	••••	••••
Wigeon	•••		•••	••••
Shoveler	•••		•••	••••
Tufted Duck	••••	••••	••••	••••
Pochard	••		•••	••••
Goldeneye	•••		•	••••
Ruddy Duck	•		•	•
Goosander				•••
Greylag Goose	••••	••••	••••	••••
Canada Goose	••••	••••	••••	••••
Mute Swan	••••	••••	••••	••••
Sparrowhawk	•••	••	•••	•••
Hobby		•	•	
Kestrel	••••	••••	••••	••••
Red-legged Partridge	•••	•••	•••	•••
Partridge	•	•	•	•
Pheasant	•••	•••	•••	•••
Water Rail	•			••
Moorhen	••••	••••	••••	••••
Coot	••••	••••	••••	••••
Lapwing	••••	•••	••••	••••
Ringed Plover	••	••	••	
Little Ringed Plover	••	•••	••	
Golden Plover	•			•
Snipe	••		••	••
Common Sandpiper	••	•••	••••	
Redshank	•••	•••	•••	
Greenshank			•	••
Dunlin	••	•	••	
Gt Black-backed Gull	•		•	•••
Lesser "	•••	•	•••	•••
Herring Gull	•••		••	•••
Common Gull	•••		•••	••••
Little Gull		•		
Black-headed Gull	••••	••••	••••	••••
Black Tern		•		
Common Tern	••	•••	•••	
Arctic Tern	•	•		
Stock Dove	••••	••••	••••	••••
Woodpigeon	••••	••••	••••	••••
Turtle Dove			••	••
Collard Dove	••••	••••	••••	••••
Cuckoo	•••	••••	•	
Little Owl	•••	•••	•••	•••
Swift		••••	•••	
Kingfisher	••	••	••	••
Green Woodpecker	••••	••••	••••	••••
Gt Spotted Woodpecker	••	••	••	••
Lesser "	•	•	•	•
Skylark	••••	••••	••••	••••

Species	Mar-April	May-June	July-Oct	Nov-Feb
Swallow	••	••••	•••	
House Martin	••	••••	•••	
Sand Martin	•••	••••	•••	
Carrion Crow	••••	••••	••••	••••
Rook	••••	••••	••••	••••
Jackdaw	••••	••••	••••	••••
Magpie	••••	••••	••••	••••
Great Tit	••••	••••	••••	••••
Blue Tit	••••	••••	••••	••••
Willow Tit	•		•	•
Long-tailed Tit	••••	••••	••••	••••
Treecreeper	•	•	•	•
Wren	••••	••••	••••	••••
Mistle Thrush	••••	••••	••••	••••
Fieldfare	••		••	••••
Song Thrush	••••	••••	••••	••••
Redwing	••	••••	••	••••
Blackbird	••••	••••	••••	••••
Wheatear	••	•	••	
Whinchat		•	•	
Robin	••••	••••	••••	••••
Reed Warbler		••••	••••	
Sedge Warbler	••	••••	•••	
Blackcap	••	••••	••••	
Garden Warbler		•••	••	
Whitethroat	•	••••	•••	
Lesser Whitethroat		••••	•••	
Willow Warbler	••	••••	•••	
Chiffchaff	•••	••••	••••	
Goldcrest	••		••	••
Spotted Flycatcher		•••	•••	
Dunnock	••••	••••	••••	••••
Meadow Pipit	••••	••••	••••	••••
Pied Wagtail	••••	••••	••••	••••
Grey Wagtail	•		•	•
Yellow Wagtail	••	••••	•••	
Starling	••••	••••	••••	••••
Greenfinch	••••	••••	••••	••••
Goldfinch	••••	••••	••••	••••
Linnet	••	••	••	••
Redpoll	•	•	•	•
Siskin	•			••
Bullfinch	••••	••••	••••	••••
Chaffinch	••••	••••	••••	••••
Brambling	•			•
Corn Bunting	•	•	•	•
Yellowhammer	••••	••••	••••	••••
Reed Bunting	••••	••••	••••	•••
House Sparrow	••••	••••	••••	••••
Tree Sparrow	••••	••••	••••	••••

Recent rarities include:- Red-necked Grebe, Mandarin Duck, Short-eared Owl, Ring Ouzel

Key: ••••   Normally present/more than 90% of time
       •••   Frequently present/50%-90% of time
       ••   Less common/10-50% of time
       •   Scarce/less than 10% of time but not a rarity

Costessey Pits

Costessey Pits are to be found 10 minutes drive to the west of Norwich City Centre. Former gravel workings, Costessey Pits are small waterbodies surrounded and well-sheltered by secondary woodland of oak and birch with an understorey of bramble and bracken.

This is the kind of place where you can drop in for half an hour and quickly find most of the birds that are present or, on a sunny day in spring, spend a couple of leisurely hours picnicking by the waterside with the offchance of seeing a kingfisher.

Costessey Pits

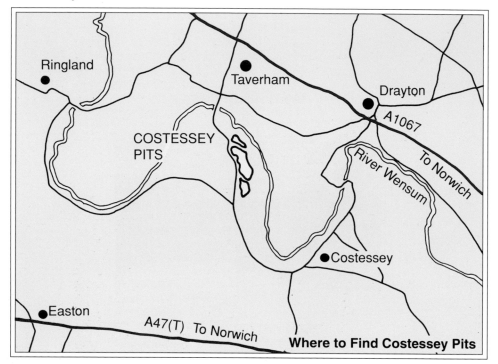

Ringland

Taverham

Drayton

A1067

COSTESSEY
PITS

River Wensum

To Norwich

Costessey

Easton

A47(T) To Norwich

Where to Find Costessey Pits

To reach Costessey Pits from Norwich take the A1067 Drayton Road out of the city and turn left for Taverham. Alternatively take the A47 Dereham Road and turn right for Costessey.

These former gravel pits play a vital role in the water supply system for Norwich. The city's water is pumped from the River Wensum into Pit 1 from which it flows into Pit 2. It is then abstracted for pumping to Heigham water treatment works where it is treated for public supply. Pit 3 is fed by natural springs. Water from Pit 3 is transferred to Pit 2. Because the three pits are linked they provide an ideal raw water storage system. They offer the flexibility of using one or more of the pits as required. They allow primary settlement to take place so water quality is uniform. This makes it easier to treat.

Enough water is stored for up to 7 days' supply, the total capacity being 280,300 cubic metres. This would safeguard the city's water supply in the event of a pollution incident requiring the river intake to be shut down.

Costessey Pits also provide an attractive local amenity. They are open to the public all year round and you will find pleasant picnic areas and good off-road car parking. Waymarked footpaths guide you through mixed woodlands by the water's edge (follow the yellow arrows). Some 1600 additional trees and shrubs have been planted, mainly native species to increase the wildlife value of the site.

Coarse angling is popular on Pits 2 and 3 but you will need a day permit. These are available in local tackle shops. If you have any fishing enquiries please contact the Secretary of the Norwich and District Anglers Association.

Water skiing is also enjoyed on Pit 2. It is run by Norwich Water Ski Club and The Deaf Bluebird Water Ski Club. For further information contact Anglian Water's Tourist Information Office on (078086) 321.

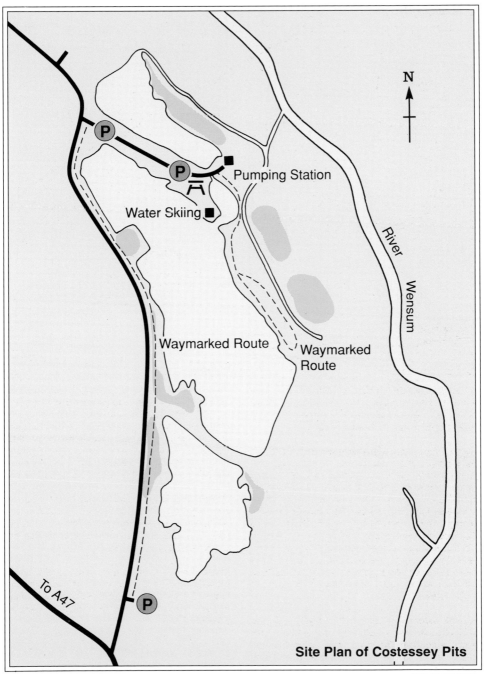

N

P

P

Pumping Station

Water Skiing ■

Waymarked Route

Waymarked Route

River Wensum

To A47

P

Site Plan of Costessey Pits

Key, see page 14

Costessey Pits Birdwatching Calendar

Species	Mar-April	May-June	July-Oct	Nov-Feb
Gt. Crested Grebe	••••	••••	••••	••••
Cormorant	••••	••••	••••	••••
Grey Heron	••	••	••	••
Mallard	••••	••••	••••	••••
Gadwall	••	••	••	••
Tufted Duck	••	••	••	••
Pochard	••	••	••	••
Goldeneye	••			••
Greylag Goose	••••	••••	••••	••••
Canada Goose	••••	••••	••••	••••
Mute Swan	••••	••••	••••	••••
Sparrowhawk	••	••	••	••
Pheasant	•••	•••	•••	•••
Moorhen	••••	••••	••••	••••
Coot	••••	••••	••••	••••
Oystercatcher	••		••	
Lapwing	••••	••••	••••	••••
Gt Black-backed Gull	••••	•••	•••	••••
Lesser "		••••	••••	
Herring Gull	••••	•••	•••	••••
Common Gull	••••	•••	•••	••••
Black-headed Gull	••••	••••	••••	••••
Black Tern		••		
Common Tern		••••	•••	
Woodpigeon	••••	••••	••••	••••
Turtle Dove		•••	•••	
Collard Dove	••••	••••	••••	••••
Cuckoo		•••	••	
Swift		••••	••••	
Kingfisher	•	•	•	•
Green Woodpecker	•	•	•	•
Gt Spotted Woodpecker	••	••	••	••
Lesser "				•
Swallow		••••	••••	
House Martin		••••	••••	
Sand Martin		••••	•••	
Carrion Crow	••••	••••	••••	••••
Rook	••••	••••	••••	••••
Jackdaw	••••	••••	••••	••••
Magpie	••••	••••	••••	••••
Jay	••••	••••	••••	••••
Great Tit	••••	••••	••••	••••
Blue Tit	••••	••••	••••	••••
Marsh Tit	•••	•••	•••	•••
Willow Tit	••			••
Long-tailed Tit	•••	•••		•••
Nuthatch	••			••
Treecreeper	•	•	•	•
Wren	••••	••••	••••	••••
Mistle Thrush	••			••
Fieldfare	••			••
Song Thrush	••••	••••	••••	••••
Redwing	••			••
Blackbird	••••	••••	••••	••••
Nightingale		••		
Robin	••••	••••	••••	••••
Reed Warbler		•••		
Sedge Warbler		••••	••••	
Blackcap		••••	••••	
Garden Warbler		•••	•••	
Whitethroat		•••	•••	
Willow Warbler		••••	••••	
Chiffchaff		••••	••••	
Goldcrest		•••	•••	
Spotted Flycatcher		••	••	
Dunnock	••••	••••	••••	••••
Pied Wagtail	••••	••••	••••	••••
Starling	••••	••••	••••	••••
Greenfinch	••••	•••	•••	••••
Goldfinch	•••	•••	•••	•••
Linnet	•••	•••	•••	•••
Redpoll	•••			•••
Bullfinch	•••			•••
Chaffinch	••••	••••	••••	••••
Brambling	••			
Yellowhammer	•••	••	••	•••
Reed Bunting	••••	••••	••••	••••
House Sparrow	••••	••••	••••	••••

Recent rarities include:- Scaup, Long-eared Owl

Key: •••• Normally present/more than 90% of time
••• Frequently present/50%-90% of time
•• Less common/10-50% of time
• Scarce/less than 10% of time but not a rarity

Birdwatching at Costessey Pits

You can park in trimly laid-out bays overlooking the water and take a meandering stroll along a short but well-defined circular route through the woods. This is often the more interesting area for birds as wildfowl numbers tend to be small and mainly comprise mallard, greylags and Canada geese. This doesn't mean you should ignore the water entirely - Costessey Pits are one of the few Anglian Water reservoirs where you have a reasonable chance of seeing kingfishers, while spring passage brings common terns and, usually, a few black terns as well.

Though small in extent, the broadleaved woodland attracts a wide variety of birds including the three woodpeckers, marsh and willow tits and nuthatches. Probably none of these birds breeds regularly on the site but all find it offers useful foraging opportunities. A reasonable number of migrants are present in summer including blackcap and spotted flycatcher in the wood and, of course, swallows, house and sand martins and swifts all hawking for insects over the open water.

Despite the spelling, the site name is pronounced "Cozzie", as in Australian for swimwear.

Covenham Reservoir

The reservoir is situated near the villages of Covenham St Bartholomew and Covenham St Mary and is close to the Louth Canal.

The reservoir forms a prominent feature in the surrounding flat, north Lincolnshire landscape. It is an embanked reservoir up to about 15 metres deep. From the air the reservoir appears square with the high embankments tapering into the adjacent farmland.

Covenham Reservoir

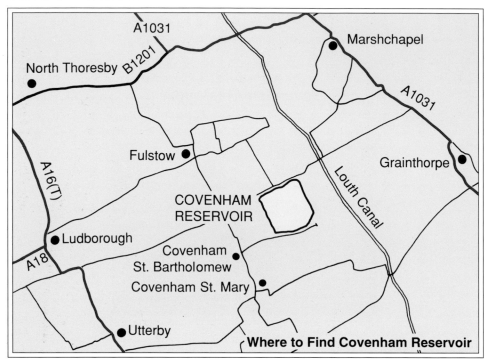

Where to Find Covenham Reservoir

Covenham reservoir can be approached from either the A16(T) Grimsby to Louth road near Ludborough or from the A1031 coastal road near Marshchapel. Parking is available alongside the north- west edge of the reservoir.

Constructed in 1970 this 88 hectare reservoir has a capacity of 10,900,000 cubic metres. It supplies water to the Cleethorpes and Grimsby areas. Water is pumped to the reservoir from the Louth Canal. After storage in the reservoir the water is treated at the adjacent Covenham water treatment works. The inside edges of the reservoir embankments are lined with concrete to protect them from erosion through wave action. This limits the growth of aquatic and marginal plants but despite this the reservoir attracts good numbers of wintering wildfowl and other water and waterside birds.

Alongside good birdwatching, sailing, water skiing and diving are on offer. These activities are run by the Covenham Water Sports Association.

A footpath runs around the reservoir and a bird hide has been built in the south-east corner overlooking an area which has been set aside for conservation.

Birdwatching at Covenham

It is rare to see long-tailed ducks inland but at this site small numbers - usually less that 10 - are often present from November to March. Normally wintering off the coast, and quite scarce south of the Moray Firth in Scotland, they are always easy to overlook and can be hard to watch. They are quite small and their grey and white plumage blends with the dappled light on choppy waters. When they are feeding they spend much more time submerged than on the surface. The upshot is that, even when you know they are there, the birds will briefly surface and dive again before you can get the binoculars trained on them. Even here at Covenham they are tricky to find as they usually stay disobligingly near the centre of the reservoir. Like Cadney this is a large raised reservoir - a square concrete tank surrounded by steep, grassy

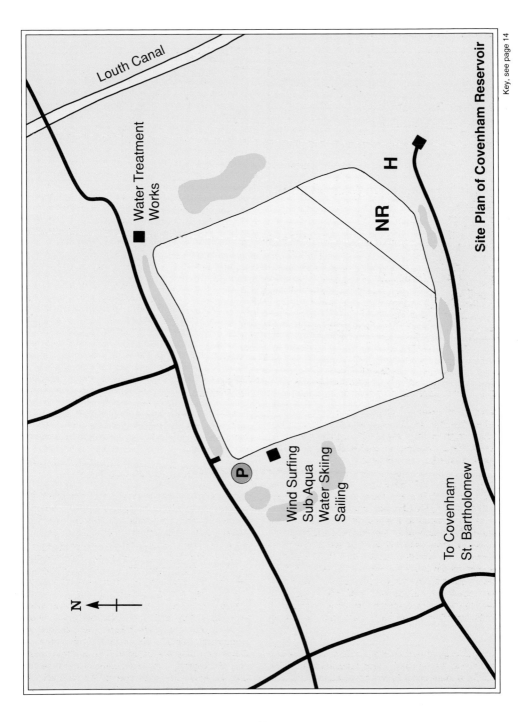

Louth Canal

Water Treatment Works

NR

H

Wind Surfing
Sub Aqua
Water Skiing
Sailing

P

To Covenham
St. Bartholomew

N

Site Plan of Covenham Reservoir

Key, see page 14

Covenham Birdwatching Calendar

Species	Mar-April	May-June	July-Oct	Nov-Feb
Gt. Crested Grebe	•••	••	•••	••••
Little Grebe	•		•	•
Cormorant	••••	••	•	••••
Grey Heron	•	•	•	•
Mallard	••••	•••	••••	••••
Teal	•••	••	••	••
Gadwall	••	•		••
Wigeon	••	•	••	•
Pintail	•		•	•
Shoveler	•	•	•	•
Tufted Duck	•••	•••	•••	•••
Pochard	••		•	••
Goldeneye	••••		••	••••
Long-tailed Duck	•••			••••
Kestrel	•••	•••	•••	•••
Moorhen	••••	••••	••••	••••
Coot	•••		••	••••
Lapwing	••		••••	••
Ringed Plover	••	••	••	
Little Ringed Plover	•	•	•	
Golden Plover	•		•	•
Green Sandpiper	••		••	••
Wood Sandpiper	•			
Common Sandpiper	••••	••••	••••	
Redshank	••		••	••
Greenshank	•	•	•	
Little Stint			•	
Dunlin	••	••	••	
Ruff	•	•	•	
Gt Black-backed Gull	••••		••••	••••
Lesser "	•		•	
Herring Gull	••••		••••	••••
Common Gull	••••		••••	••••
Black-headed Gull	••••		••••	••••
Black Tern		•		
Common Tern	••	•••	•••	
Arctic Tern	•	•	•	
Woodpigeon	••••	••••	••••	••••
Turtle Dove		•		
Collared Dove	••••	••••	••••	••••
Cuckoo		•••		
Barn Owl	•			•
Swift		•••	•••	
Skylark	•	•••	•••	
Swallow	••	••••	••••	
House Martin	••	••••	••••	
Sand Martin	•	•	•	
Carrion Crow	••••	••••	••••	••••
Rook	••••	••••	••••	••••
Jackdaw	••	••	••	••
Magpie	••••	••••	••••	••••
Mistle Thrush	•			•
Fieldfare	•			•
Song Thrush	••	••	••	••
Redwing	•			•

Species	Mar-April	May-June	July-Oct	Nov-Feb
Blackbird	••••	••••	••••	••••
Wheatear	•	•	•	
Meadow Pipit	••••	•••	••••	•
Pied Wagtail	••••	••••	••••	•
Yellow Wagtail	••	••••	•••	
Starling	••••	••••	••••	••••
Greenfinch	••			••
Goldfinch	•	••	••	
Linnet	••	•••	••	•
Chaffinch	••			••
Yellowhammer	••			••
Reed Bunting	•	••	•	
House Sparrow	••••	••••	••••	••••

Recent rarities include:- Great Northern Diver, Slavonian Grebe, Black-winged Stilt, Glaucous Gull

Key: •••• Normally present/more than 90% of time
••• Frequently present/50%-90% of time
•• Less common/10-50% of time
• Scarce/less than 10% of time but not a rarity

embankments - and like Cadney it can be very windswept. The good news is that there is a cosy hide which gives welcome shelter while you search for the elusive long-tails. The bad news is that it is diametrically opposite the car park, about half an hours' healthful walk away.

The water area nearest the hide is a sanctuary zone and many birds move into it when sailing and waterskiing are in progress so the weekend is often the best time to visit. Waterfowl numbers vary considerably during the course of the winter - they can approach 1000 but sometimes drop to less than 300. Coot, in early winter, mallard, tufted duck and pochard are the most numerous and goldeneye numbers are good, with 50 or more present, often at close range.

Walking between carpark and hide, look out for yellow wagtails, meadow pipits and perhaps wheatear on migration in spring and autumn. There is also a reasonable wader passage. Overall interest is lowest in the summer months with perhaps no more than 20 species present, mostly in the young blocks of scrub on the embankments.

Foxcote Reservoir

Situated near Buckingham this pleasant, tranquil reservoir is an absolute haven for wildlife. In particular, the wood fringing the reservoir and the absence of watersports on the lake make the area very popular for birds. The wildlife and natural beauty of the reservoir have long been safeguarded. A nature reserve was created in 1971 when Anglian Water, in partnership with Buckinghamshire, Berkshire and Oxfordshire Naturalists Trust (BBONT), drew up a management agreement to enhance the wildlife value of the reserve.

The reservoir has since been designated as a Site of Special Scientific Interest (SSSI) to further protect the area's conservation value.

Foxcote Reservoir

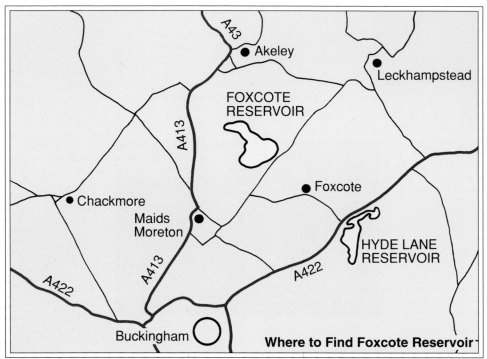

Where to Find Foxcote Reservoir

Foxcote Reservoir is situated about 1.5 kilometres north of Buckingham. Access is available via the A413 north of Buckingham off the road between Maid's Moreton and Leckhampstead. There is no official car park but there are places on the lane verges where you might leave your car.

The reservoir was formed in the 1950's by flooding a 24 hectare field. It holds 477,000 cubic metres of water and supplies customers in the towns of Buckingham and Brackley as well as villages to the north and west.

If you would like to spend an hour or two birdwatching, you need to obtain a permit which is issued by BBONT. This also allows use of the hide to the south of the site. If you simply want to enjoy the beauty of the lake most of the lake can be seen from the roadway just east of the dam and the whole reservoir can be viewed from the public footpath to Foxcote Wood. Details and permits for the nature reserve are available from BBONT, Haydon Mill, Rabans Lane, Aylesbury, Bucks. Tel (0296) 433222.

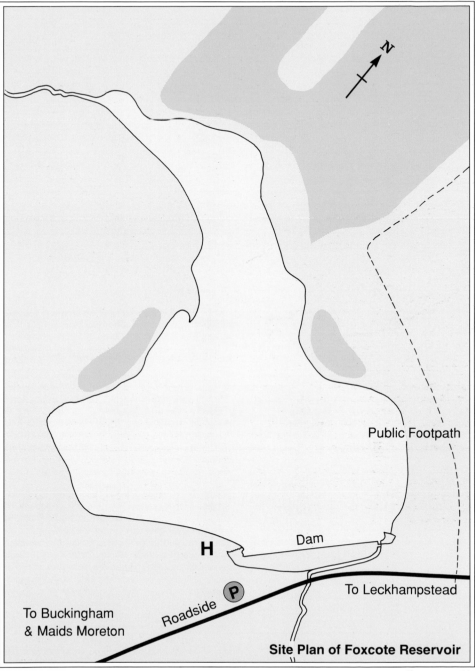

N

Public Footpath

H

Dam

To Leckhampstead

P

Roadside

To Buckingham
& Maids Moreton

Site Plan of Foxcote Reservoir

Key, see page 14

Foxcote Birdwatching Calendar

Species	Mar-April	May-June	July-Oct	Nov-Feb
Gt. Crested Grebe	••••	••••	••••	••••
Little Grebe	•••	•••	•••	•••
Cormorant	••		••	••
Grey Heron	•••	•••	•••	•••
Mallard	••••	••••	••••	••••
Teal	••••		••	••••
Wigeon	••		•	•••
Shoveler	•••		•••	••••
Tufted Duck	••••	•••	••••	••••
Pochard	••••		•••	••••
Goldeneye	••••		•••	••••
Ruddy Duck	••••		••	••••
Goosander				••
Greylag Goose				••
Canada Goose	••••	••	••••	••••
Mute Swan	••••	••••	••••	••••
Kestrel	••	••	••	••
Pheasant	•••	•••	•••	•••
Moorhen	••••	••••	••••	••••
Coot	••••	••••	••••	••••
Lapwing	•		•	•
Snipe	•		•	•
Woodcock	•	•		
Common Sandpiper			•	
Redshank	•		••	
Gt Black-backed Gull	••			••
Herring Gull	••••		•••	••••
Common Gull	••••		•••	••••
Black-headed Gull	••••		••••	••••
Stock Dove	•••	•••	•••	•••
Woodpigeon	••••	••••	••••	••••
Turtle Dove		••	•	
Cuckoo	••	••••	••	
Tawny Owl	•	•	•	•
Swift		••••	•••	
Green Woodpecker	••	•	•	••
Great Spotted "	•	•	•	•
Skylark	••		••	•
Swallow	••	••••	•••	
House Martin	••	••••	•••	
Sand Martin	•	••	•	
Carrion Crow	••••	••••	••••	••••
Rook	••••	••••	••••	••••
Jackdaw	••••	••••	••••	••••
Jay	••	••	••	••
Great Tit	••••	••••	••••	••••
Blue Tit	••••	••••	••••	••••
Marsh Tit	••	••	••	••
Long-Tailed Tit	•••	•••	•••	•••
Nuthatch	•	•	•	•
Treecreeper	••	••	••	••
Wren	••••	••••	••••	••••
Mistle Thrush	••	••	••	••
Fieldfare				•
Song Thrush	••••	••••	••••	••••
Redwing				•
Blackbird	••••	••••	••••	••••
Robin	••••	••••	••••	••••
Reed Warbler		•••	•••	
Sedge Warbler	•••	••••	•••	
Blackcap		••	••	
Garden Warbler		•	•	
Whitethroat		•••	••	
Lesser Whitethroat		•••	••	
Willow Warbler	••	••••	••••	
Chiffchaff	••	••••	••••	
Dunnock	••••	••••	••••	••••
Pied Wagtail	••••	••••	••••	••••
Starling	••••	••••	••••	••••
Greenfinch	•••	•••	•••	•••
Goldfinch	••	••	••	••
Linnet	••	••	••	••
Bullfinch	••	••	••	••
Chaffinch	••••	••••	••••	••••
Yellowhammer	••	••	••	••
Reed Bunting	•••	••••	•••	••
House Sparrow	••	•	••	••

Key: •••• Normally present/more than 90% of time
••• Frequently present/50%-90% of time
•• Less common/10-50% of time
• Scarce/less than 10% of time but not a rarity

Birdwatching at Foxcote

Screened by hill slopes and woodland, Foxcote's sheltered waters attract a wide variety of waterfowl. Birds have what seems to be a remarkable ability to find good sites but in reality it is nothing more mysterious than the fact that when you are flying high you can see any patches of open water from miles away. Foxcote must be easily visible to birds moving along the Ouse Valley to the south. Typically in the course of the winter up to 16 waterfowl species occur. They include little grebe - a surprisingly scarce bird on Anglian Water reservoirs - teal, shoveler, ruddy duck, goldeneye and goosander. The peak count is usually 400-500 birds.

Much of the bank is lined with self-sown scrub and broadleaved woodland so that the upper end in particular is very secluded. Access is restricted to one hide, on the bank at the western end of the dam. This successfully prevents disturbance but it does mean that birdwatching here requires some patience and skill. Birds like teal and shoveler, which are likely to feed and rest at the margins, can remain out of view for long periods. Patient observation is usually rewarded, but a quick visit is likely to miss species. As for woodland bird identification, that depends largely on your ability to recognise calls and songs. With these provisions, the site has a lot to offer throughout the year and even if there isn't much about, it is still a very pleasing scene to look upon!

Grafham Water

Grafham Water was opened in 1966 by HRH Prince Philip, Duke of Edinburgh, and covers an area of 600 hectares. The area was originally the shallow agricultural valley of Diddington Brook, Huntingdonshire, now part of Cambridgeshire. Water is abstracted from the River Great Ouse near Offord, about 5 kilometres upstream of Huntingdon, and pumped into the reservoir. It holds 69,000,000 cubic metres of water and forms a vital part of the strategic Ruthamford water supply network.

This system is capable of producing 640,000 cubic metres of water a day for over 1.6 million customers. The name of the system is derived from the names of its three largest reservoirs Rutland, Grafham and Pitsford.

Grafham Water

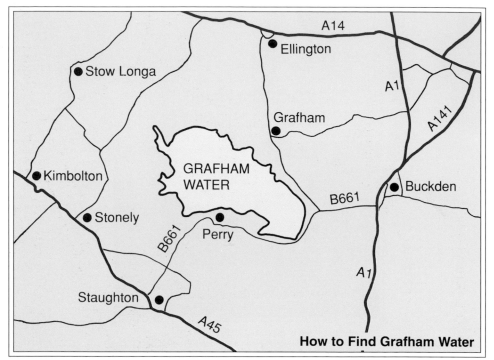

How to Find Grafham Water

Grafham Water is situated about 10 kilometres south west of Huntingdon, just 5 kilometres from the A1. Follow the signs from the roundabout at Buckden. From the west it is 64 kilometres from Northampton on the A45 or 48 kilometres from Kettering on the A14. From the east either take the M11 motorway or the A45 until you join the A1. The three car parks (Mander, Plummer and Marlow) offer splendid views of the water and all have toilets and childrens' play areas. For further details of the history and operation of the reservoir a visit to the Marlow Exhibition Centre is a must. While you are there you can pick up information on the leisure facilities and the natural history to be found at Grafham Water. Tel: (0480) 512154.

Whatever your age, Grafham Water has something to offer you. Windsurfing, cycling and adventure playgrounds will appeal to the energetic. Fly fishing and nature trails offer more leisurely exercise, whilst a quiet picnic by the water's edge or an hour's bird watching from one of the hides completes the choice. Why not hire a bike to explore the 18 kilometre circular route, opened in 1991. It joins original footpaths and bridleways, even linking to long distance routes, such as the Three Shires Way. Please keep to the paths in the nature reserve at the western end of the reservoir to keep disturbance to wildlife to a minimum. Grafham Water is a popular place for dinghy sailing and windsurfing throughout the week. It is regularly the venue for Olympic trials and National Championships but the beginner is always welcome and professional coaching is available. You will find the club house on the south shore and day membership is available. For further details of this and coaching telephone (0480) 810478. Rescue services are maintained by the Grafham Water Sailing Club whenever sailing takes place.

Also located at Perry is the Grafham Water Centre. Students can be accommodated for courses related to water sports and environmental studies throughout the summer. During the remainder of the year you can take courses in Music, Drama, Languages and Creative Arts. Details of all courses are available from the Warden on (0480) 810521.

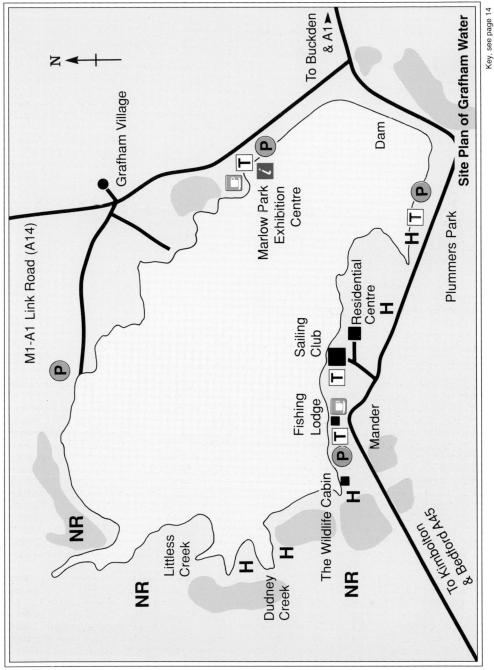

Site Plan of Grafham Water

Key, see page 14

N

M1-A1 Link Road (A14)

Gratham Village

To Buckden & A1 ▶

P

T

i

Marlow Park Exhibition Centre

Dam

P

Plummers Park

H T

Residential Centre

H

Sailing Club

Fishing Lodge

T

Mander

P T

The Wildlife Cabin

H

NR

Littless Creek

NR

Dudney Creek

H

H

NR

To Kimbolton & Bedford A45

Internationally renowned amongst anglers, Grafham enjoys a reputation for producing huge trout. It regularly hosts local and national events and played host to the 1987 World Championships. Permits are available for day, season or evenings with 50% reductions for juniors aged 16 or less. Fishing is by fly only. If you are interested in learning to fly fish, Grafham offers a range of courses and beginner's weeks to suit your needs. Boat fishing usually gives the biggest catches. You can hire one of the fleet of powered dinghies available at the Fishing Lodge, Mander Car Park, West Perry. The Lodge has a licensed catering service which provides breakfasts, lunches and evening meals. Special arrangements can be made for events. There is also a well stocked tackle shop which is open every day throughout the trout season. If you have any fishing enquiries contact the Fishing Lodge, West Perry, Huntingdon, Cambs PE18 OBX. Tel. (0480) 810531. The fishery wardens and angling instructor are always pleased to advise.

For further information about Grafham Water and its facilities or indeed any of our reservoirs please contact Anglian Water Tourist Information Centre on (078086) 321.

Birdwatching at Grafham Water

You can tackle Grafham Water on a number of different levels of exertion all of which have their merits, depending on how energetic you feel and the state of the weather. The simplest is to drive to Mander carpark, visit the reserve warden's office to find out what's about and then either stroll into the reserve - the nearest hide is only 100 yards away - or take your car to whichever other area sounds promising. At the other extreme, Grafham is the right size to walk all round in half a day, though if you are birding it is likely to take you 5 - 6 hours.

Usually the two most rewarding areas are the reserve and the sludge lagoons. In the reserve, the first hide has disabled access. Bird numbers at this point tend to be small, however. Much bigger waterfowl concentrations develop in Littless creek and Dudney creek as this is the sanctuary zone into which birds retreat when disturbed by boats and bankside recreation.

The reserve also contains several areas of woodland planted about 20 years ago, two blocks of older timber - Littless Wood and Savages Spinney - and patches of self-sown scrub. Overall,

it holds quite a rich assemblage of birds including turtledove, grasshopper warbler, nightingale, long-eared owl, sparrowhawk and woodcock. Yellow wagtails are widespread on the grassland areas.

The sludge lagoons adjacent to East Perry are overlooked by a hide which is always worth visiting. Some lagoons are shallowly flooded, attracting teal and shoveler in winter and shelducks in the breeding season. When first drained the "mudflats" are used by snipe, redshank and other waders. Those that dry out completely may hold breeding ringed and little ringed plover and lapwing. Several of the lagoons have become well-vegetated habitat for water rail and reed warbler. There is nothing but great self-restraint to prevent you walking all round the perimeter of this rich area and it is very tempting to do so but it causes great disturbance to wildfowl and waders, plus annoyance to people still in the hide.

There is one more hide, overlooking Gaynes Cove. Like the first hide in the reserve, this too has disabled access and can be very good for a wide variety of wintering wildfowl.

Total numbers of winter wildfowl have been disappointing in the last couple of years but you still have a good chance of seeing a dozen or more species in a visit. There is a massive winter gull roost which can include rare species, if you have the skill and patience to pick them out. Otherwise their evening arrival is a good spectacle anyway. Migration seasons are always rewarding but, of course, chancey. What you see, if anything, is a matter of luck. A total of over 20 wader species, Arctic and black terns, little gull, Arctic skua and osprey are usually recorded.

If you visit Grafham Water regularly, you will certainly find that you need a telescope. Its size and shape mean that birds like divers can be too far off-shore for certain identification with binoculars alone.

Grafham Birdwatching Calendar

Species	Mar-April	May-June	July-Oct	Nov-Feb
Gt. Crested Grebe	••••	••••	••••	••••
Little Grebe	••	•	•	••
Cormorant	••••	••••	••••	••••
Grey Heron	••••	••••	••••	••••
Mallard	••••	••••	••••	••••
Teal	••••	•	•••	••••
Gadwall	••••	•••	••••	••••
Wigeon	••••		••	••••
Shoveler	••••	•	•••	••••
Tufted Duck	••••	•••	••••	••••
Pochard	••••	•	•••	••••
Goldeneye	•			•••
Ruddy Duck				•
Goosander				•••
Shelduck	••••	••••	•••	••
Greylag Goose	•	•	•	•
Mute Swan	•••	•••	•••	•••
Sparrowhawk	•	•	•	•
Hobby			•	
Kestrel	••••	••••	••••	••••
Red-legged Partridge	•	•	•	•
Pheasant	••••	••••	••••	••••
Moorhen	••••	••••	••••	••••
Coot	••••	••••	••••	••••
Lapwing	••••	••••	••••	••••
Ringed Plover	•••	•••	•••	
Little Ringed Plover	••	•••	••	
Golden Plover				•
Snipe				•••
Woodcock		•		
Fieldfare			••	••
Song Thrush	••••	••••	••••	••••
Redwing			••	••
Blackbird	••••	••••	••••	••••
Wheatear	•		•	
Nightingale		••		
Robin	••••	••••	••••	••••
Grasshopper Warbler		••		
Reed Warbler	••	•••	••	
Sedge Warbler	••	•••	••	
Blackcap		•••	••	
Garden Warbler		•••	••	
Whitethroat		•••	••	
Lesser Whitethroat		•••	••	
Willow Warbler	•••	••••	••••	
Chiffchaff	•••	••••	•••	
Goldcrest	••	••	••	••
Spotted Flycatcher		••	••	
Dunnock	••••	••••	••••	••••
Meadow Pipit	••		••	••
Pied Wagtail	••••	••••	••••	••••
Yellow Wagtail		••••	•••	
Starling	••••	••••	••••	••••
Little Owl	•	•	•	•
Tawny Owl	•			•
Swift		••••	••••	

Species	Mar-April	May-June	July-Oct	Nov-Feb
Green Woodpecker	•	•	•	•
Great Spotted "	•	•	•	•
Skylark	•••	•••	•••	•••
Swallow	•••	••••	••••	
House Martin	•••	••••	••••	
Sand Martin	•••	••	•••	
Carrion Crow	••••	••••	••••	••••
Rook	••••	••••	••••	••••
Jackdaw	••••	••••	••••	••••
Magpie	••	••	••	••
Jay	••	••	••	••
Great Tit	••••	••••	••••	••••
Blue Tit	••••	••••	••••	••••
Marsh Tit	••	••	••	•
Willow Tit	•	•	•	•
Long-tailed Tit	•••	•••	•••	•••
Treecreeper	•	•	•	•
Wren	••••	••••	••••	••••
Mistle Thrush	•••	•••	•••	•••
Common Sandpiper	•		••	
Redshank	••••	••••	••••	••••
Greenshank			••	
Little Stint			•	
Dunlin			••	••
Ruff			•	
Gt Black-backed Gull	••••		•••	••••
Lesser Black-backed Gull	••••		••••	••
Herring Gull	••••	•••	••••	••••
Common Gull	••••		••••	••••
Little Gull		•	•	
Black-headed Gull	••••	•••	••••	••••
Black Tern		•	•	
Common Tern		••••	••••	
Arctic Tern		•	•	
Stock Dove	••••	••••	••••	••••
Woodpigeon	••••	••••	••••	••••
Turtle Dove		••••	•••	
Collard Dove	••	••	••	••
Cuckoo	•••	••••	•••	
Greenfinch	•••	•••	•••	•••
Goldfinch	••	•••	••••	
Linnet	•••	•••	•••	•••
Redpoll	•	•	•	•
Bullfinch	••	••	••	•••
Chaffinch	••••	••••	••••	••••
Yellowhammer	••••	••••	••••	••••
Reed Bunting	••••	••••	••••	••••
House Sparrow	••••	••••	••••	••••

Recent rarities include:- Leach's Petrel, Surf Scooter, Pomarine Skua, Ring-billed Gull, Waxwing, Bluethroat

Key: •••• Normally present/more than 90% of time
  ••• Frequently present/50%-90% of time
  •• Less common/10-50% of time
  • Scarce/less than 10% of time but not a rarity

Hollowell Reservoir

Hollowell Reservoir nestles in a narrow sheltered valley 16 kilometres north-west of Northampton.

The reservoir became operational in 1938 and holds over 2,091,000 cubic metres of water. Although it isn't a large site, Hollowell has a good species list and it turns up a wide variety of uncommon birds each year.

Hollowell Reservoir

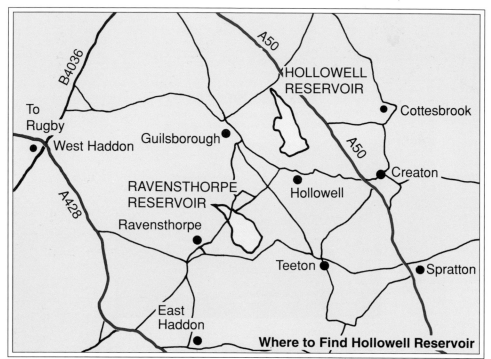

Where to Find Hollowell Reservoir

Access to Hollowell reservoir from the M1 motorway (10 kilometres away) is from Junction 18 at Crick. Follow the A428 to West Haddon then turn left towards Cold Ashby on the B4036. Turn right towards Guilsborough and go through the village to Hollowell. You will find car parks at the northern end of the reservoir on the road between Guilsborough village and the A50 and also at the top of the access road to the Sailing Club between the villages of Guilsborough and Hollowell.

Covering 54 hectares Hollowell boasts a thriving sailing club. The club is based at the western end of the dam. Although day sailing is not available, club membership is inexpensive and there are now over 200 craft in the club's fleet of dinghies and sailboards. Applications for membership should be sent to the Secretary, Hollowell Sailing Club, Hollowell, Northamptonshire.

Hollowell Reservoir also boasts a specimen coarse fishery. It has a reputation for big roach, rudd, carp, tench, perch and pike which grow to over 30 pounds here. Day and season permits are available in advance from the Fishing Lodge at Pitsford Water on (0604) 781350.

If you feel like horse riding or birdwatching then these permits are also issued from Pitsford Fishing Lodge at Holcot only a few miles away.

If you have enjoyed your visit to Hollowell why not call in at Ravensthorpe Reservoir (5 minutes drive away) or visit Pitsford Water? Bird watching permits are easily available from the Pitsford Fishing Lodge.

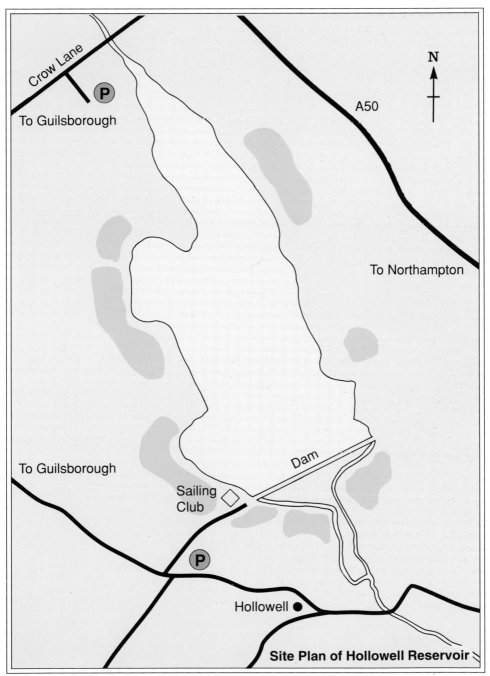

Crow Lane

To Guilsborough

P

N

A50

To Northampton

To Guilsborough

Dam

Sailing
Club

P

Hollowell ●

Site Plan of Hollowell Reservoir

Key, see page 14

57

Birdwatching at Hollowell

The early part of the winter usually brings quite large numbers of gadwall, shoveler and teal, all of which feed mainly in the shallows especially adjacent to the marshy margins on the western side. From midwinter, this is a good site for goosander with 10 to 20 individuals present until late February. Maximum wildfowl numbers are usually a bit under one thousand birds. Most of these are Canada geese, mallard and coot but there can be a dozen other species present in addition.

There are no hides and no sanctuary area. As the site is used for sailing and fishing, disturbance pressure on birds can be quite heavy at times so it's important not to needlessly add to it by scaring birds out of quiet corners while trying to see what is present. This can be a bit of a problem. It is probably best to first follow the path from the main car park to the dam. From here you should see much of what's on the open water. Which bank you follow from there will depend on light conditions. The west side is often better in this respect. Though part of it is wooded, there are several rides which lead to secluded bays. Careful approach is necessary to avoid putting birds to flight. The woodlands are mostly conifer plantations and undergrazing by sheep reduces their potential for birds but the usual commoner songbirds are present and crossbill and siskin are recorded occasionally.

You can also approach the site from the car park at the north end. Birding as you go, the complete circuit on foot is likely to take at least an hour and probably nearer two.

Hollowell Birdwatching Calendar

Species	Mar-April	May-June	July-Oct	Nov-Feb
Gt. Crested Grebe	••••	••••	••••	••••
Little Grebe	••••	••	••••	•••
Grey Heron	•••	••	••	•••
Mallard	••••	••••	••••	••••
Teal	••••			••••
Gadwall	••	•	•	•••
Wigeon	••••			••••
Pintail	•			•
Shoveler	••			•••
Tufted Duck	••••	••••	••••	••••
Pochard	•••		•	••••
Goldeneye	••••			••••
Ruddy Duck	••••	••	••	••••
Goosander				•
Greylag Goose	•••	•••	•••	••••
Canada Goose	••••	••••	••••	••••
Mute Swan	••••	••••	••••	••••
Sparrowhawk	••	••	••	••
Kestrel	•	•	•	•
Red-legged Partridge	•	•	•	•
Pheasant	•••	•••	•••	•••
Moorhen	••••	••••	••••	••••
Coot	••••	••••	••••	••••
Lapwing	•••	•	•••	••••
Ringed Plover			•	
Little Ringed Plover		••	•	
Golden Plover			•	•
Snipe	••		•	••
Common Sandpiper	••		••	
Redshank			•	
Greenshank			•	
Dunlin			•	
Ruff			•	
Gt Black-backed Gull				•
Lesser "	••	•	••	••
Herring Gull			••	
Common Gull	••		••	••••
Black-headed Gull	••••		•••	••••
Black Tern		•		
Common Tern	••	••	••	
Arctic Tern	•			
Stock Dove	••	••	••	••
Woodpigeon	••••	••••	••••	••••
Turtle Dove		••	•	
Collard Dove	•	•	•	•
Cuckoo	•	•••	•	
Tawny Owl	•••	•••	•••	•••
Swift		••••	•••	
Green Woodpecker	••	••	••	••
Great Spotted "	•••	•••	•••	•••
Swallow		••••	••••	
House Martin		••••	••••	
Sand Martin	•	••	••	
Carrion Crow	••••	••••	••••	••••
Rook	••••	••••	••••	••••
Jackdaw	••••	••••	••••	••••

Species	Mar-April	May-June	July-Oct	Nov-Feb
Magpie	••	••	••	••
Jay	•			•
Great Tit	••••	••••	••••	••••
Blue Tit	••••	••••	••••	••••
Coal Tit	••••	••••	••••	••••
Marsh Tit	••••	••••	••••	••••
Willow Tit	•	•	•	•
Long-tailed Tit	•••	•••	•••	•••
Treecatcher	••	••	••	••
Wren	••••	••••	••••	••••
Mistle Thrush	••	••	••	••
Fieldfare	••			•••
Song Thrush	••••	••••	••••	••••
Redwing	••			•••
Blackbird	••••	••••	••••	••••
Robin	••••	••••	••••	••••
Reed Warbler			••	••
Blackcap	•••	••••	•••	
Garden Warbler		•	•	
Whitethroat		•	•	
Lesser Whitethroat		••	••	
Willow Warbler	•••	••••	•••	
Chiffchaff	•••	••••	•••	
Goldcrest	••••	•••	•••	••••
Spotted Flycatcher		••	••	
Dunnock	••••	••••	••••	••••
Meadow Pipit				••
Pied Wagtail	••••	••••	••••	••••
Yellow Wagtail	••	••	••	
Starling	••••	••••	••••	••••
Greenfinch	••••	••••	••••	••••
Goldfinch	•••	•••	•••	•••
Linnet	••	••	••	••
Redpoll	••		•	••
Bullfinch	•••	•••	•••	•••
Chaffinch	••••	••••	••••	••••
Brambling	•			•
Yellowhammer	••••	••••	••••	••••
Reed Bunting	••••	••••	••••	••••
House Sparrow	••••	••••	••••	••••
Tree Sparrow	•	•	•	•

Recent rarities include:- Common Scoter, Smew, Osprey, Pectoral Sandpiper, Rock Pipit

Key: •••• Normally present/more than 90% of time
••• Frequently present/50%-90% of time
•• Less common/10-50% of time
• Scarce/less than 10% of time but not a rarity

59

Hyde Lane Reservoir

Hyde Lane lies north-east of Buckingham, off the A422 towards North Milton Keynes. The lake is visible from the road and access to restricted parking at the southernmost tip of the lake is via a rough track.

The lake's role centres on a pumped storage facility. When the need arises, water can be fed from the Great Ouse River into the lake, and transferred to nearby Foxcote reservoir for water supply to the local area. The 136,000 cubic metre capacity lake also offers opportunities for recreation and conservation

Hyde Lane Reservoir

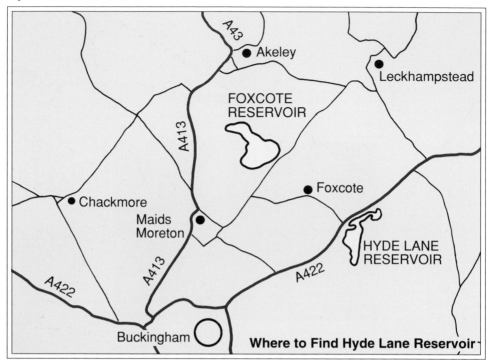

Where to Find Hyde Lane Reservoir

This scenic waterbody is small, but intricately shaped with bays and inlets characterising the shoreline. A small area of mature woodland lends valuable wildlife habitat and means that the lake provides good birdwatching. The southern fringe of the lake is a nature reserve run by the Buckinghamshire, Berkshire and Oxfordshire Naturalists Trust (BBONT). This area, between the lake and the public footpath, was once part of the Buckingham Canal, and was obtained by the Trust to protect the aquatic fauna in the canal's remnant pools. Coarse fishing is also popular at the lake. Details are available from the Buckingham and District Angling Society or from the Anglian Water Tourist Information Centre on (078086) 321.

Birdwatching at Hyde Lane

Perhaps this isn't much of a place for really keen birders. It doesn't hold big numbers of birds and it doesn't attract many rarities. It has the informal charm shared by all old gravel pits abandoned to nature. Grass grows tall and tussocky, scrub springs up self-sown, willows and alders colonise

the banks and beds of reedmace advance across the shallows. Lots of small birds find these conditions very congenial - sedge warbler and willow warblers, long-tailed tit, bullfinch, goldfinch and linnet, yellowhammer and reed bunting. All common birds but well worth a second look on purely aesthetic grounds.

What's more, if you want to learn birdsong it is always wise to start in a place like this where the range of species is not too great and you can normally see what is making the sound.

Hyde Lane has coarse fishing from June through to March but in the breeding season, when birdsong is at its height, the site is little disturbed.

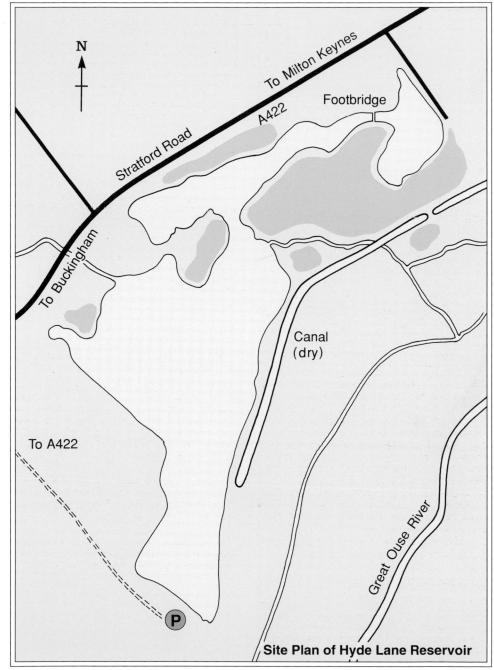

Site Plan of Hyde Lane Reservoir

N

To Milton Keynes

A422

Stratford Road

Footbridge

To Buckingham

To A422

Canal (dry)

Great Ouse River

P

Key, see page 14

Hyde Lane Birdwatching Calendar

Species	Mar-April	May-June	July-Oct	Nov-Feb
Gt. Crested Grebe	••••	••••	••••	••••
Little Grebe		•	•	
Cormorant	••		••	••
Grey Heron	•••	•••	•••	•••
Mallard	••••	••••	••••	••••
Tufted Duck	••••	•	•••	••••
Pochard	•••		••	•••
Canada Goose	••	••	••	••
Mute Swan	••	••	••	••
Sparrowhawk	•	•	•	•
Kestrel	•	•	•	•
Pheasant	•••	•••	•••	•••
Moorhen	••••	••••	••••	••••
Coot	••••	••••	••••	••••
Snipe	•			•
Green Sandpiper			•	
Common Sandpiper	•		••	
Redshank				•
Herring Gull				•
Black-headed Gull	•••		•••	••••
Stock Dove	•••	•••	•••	•••
Woodpigeon	••••	••••	••••	••••
Turtle Dove		••	••	
Cuckoo		••	•	
Swift		••••	•••	
Gt Spotted Woodpecker	••	••	••	••
Lesser "		•		
Swallow	••	••••	••••	
House Martin	••	••••	••••	
Sand Martin	•	••	••	
Carrion Crow	••••	••••	••••	••••
Rook	••••	••••	••••	••••
Jackdaw	••••	••••	••••	••••
Magpie	••	••	••	••
Great Tit	••••	••••	••••	••••
Blue Tit	••••	••••	••••	••••
Willow Tit	•	•	•	•
Long-tailed Tit	••	••	••	••
Wren	••••	••••	••••	••••
Mistle Thrush	••	••	••	••
Fieldfare				•
Song Thrush	•••	•••	•••	•••
Redwing				•
Blackbird	••••	••••	••••	••••
Robin	••••	••••	••••	••••
Sedge Warbler		••••	•••	
Whitethroat		••	•	
Lesser Whitethroat		•	•	
Willow Warbler	••	••••	•••	
Chiffchaff	••		••	
Dunnock	••••	••••	••••	••••
Pied Wagtail	••••	••••	••••	••••
Starling	••••	••••	••••	••••
Greenfinch	•••	•••	•••	••
Goldfinch	••	•••	•••	•
Linnet	••	••	••	••

Species				
Bullfinch	•••	•••	•••	•••
Chaffinch	••••	••••	••••	••••
Yellowhammer	•••	•••	•••	•••
Reed Bunting	••••	••••	••••	••••
House Sparrow	•••	•••	•••	•••

Key: •••• Normally present/more than 90% of time
••• Frequently present/50%-90% of time
•• Less common/10-50% of time
• Scarce/less than 10% of time but not a rarity

Pitsford Water

Pitsford Water lies in rolling countryside just north of Northampton.

This impounding reservoir was formed by an earth embankment across a tributary of the River Nene. Construction of the reservoir began in 1952 and the water treatment works was opened by HM The Queen Mother in October 1956. The works supplies 45,000 cubic metres of water to the Ruthamford water supply network daily.

Pitsford Water

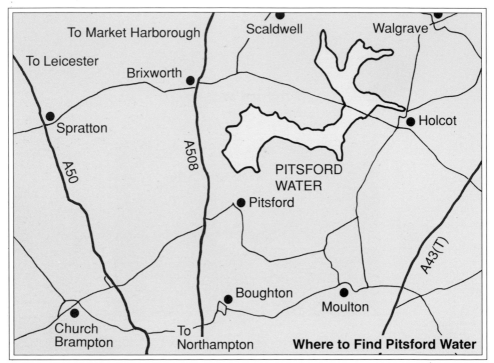

To Market Harborough

To Leicester

Scaldwell

Walgrave

Brixworth

Spratton

A50

A508

Holcot

PITSFORD
WATER

Pitsford

A43(T)

Boughton

Moulton

Church
Brampton

To
Northampton

Where to Find Pitsford Water

Pitsford Water can easily be reached from the A43 Northampton - Kettering road (via Holcot) and the A508 Northampton - Market Harborough road (via Pitsford village or Brixworth). There is ample public car parking either at the opposite end of the causeway to the fishing lodge or near the dam by Pitsford village - the latter has toilets.

There is plenty to do at Pitsford Water. You can walk on the waymarked routes between the dam and causeway though access to the Nature reserve is restricted to permit holders only. This helps keep disturbance to wildlife to a minimum. The wooded shores of Pitsford provide an attractive setting for birdwatching and horseriding. Permits for these activities can be obtained from the Fishing Lodge at Holcot. But if you just want to relax why not sit and enjoy waterside views while having a picnic at one of the areas provided at the above car parks.

Almost 200 hectares of Pitsford Water are available for sailing. Northampton Sailing Club have their clubhouse and moorings at the Brixworth end of the dam with access off the A508

just north of Pitsford Village. The club has over 300 craft. Racing and casual sailing take place mostly at weekends but also on summer evenings. For more information contact the Secretary, Northampton Sailing Club, Pitsford Water, Northampton.

As one of the most popular game fisheries in the Midlands, Pitsford Water offers excellent facilities. The fishery is regularly stocked with good quality brown and rainbow trout which have a reputation for surface feeding as the reservoir is relatively shallow. Traditional dry fly and loch style drifting from boats are therefore very effective. You can hire motor boats. Permits are available at the Fishing Lodge together with information on a range of fly fishing courses which cater for beginners as well as the more experienced angler. The season runs from the beginning of April (or Easter) to 31st December each year. If you want details of courses, to buy fishing tackle, or just need further information then call the Fishing Lodge, Pitsford Water, Brixworth Road, Holcot, Northampton NN6 9SJ. Tel. (0604) 781350.

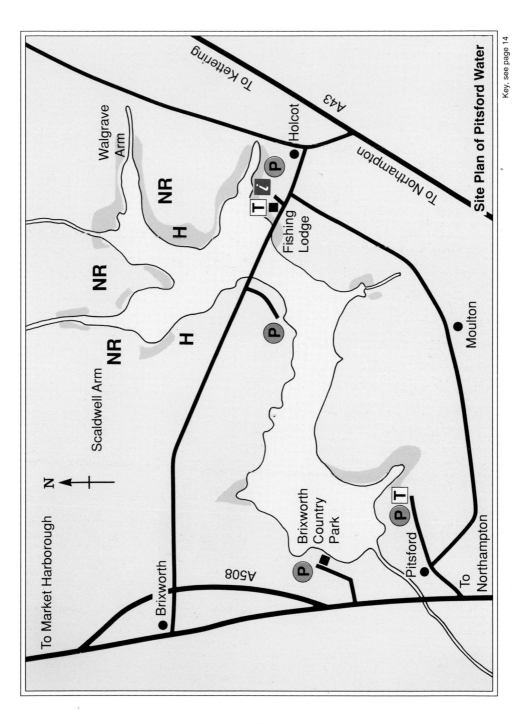

Site Plan of Pitsford Water

Key, see page 14

Birdwatching at Pitsford Water

While you can get quite good winter birdwatching from a brief stop on the causeway which crosses the site - often without even getting out of your car - Pitsford really merits a more wholehearted approach.

Almost all the area north of the causeway is nature reserve and it can be very rewarding to make the complete circuit of both the Walgrave Arm and the Scaldwell Arm as large numbers of birds can be tucked away here. A compromise is to take the 20-30 minute walk up to one or other of the hides, perhaps choosing the east bank in the morning or the west bank later in the day, in order to have the light at your back. Both hides are perched on stilts so they give first-rate views right across to the opposite shore.

By mid-September waterfowl numbers have usually already passed 3,000 birds and in mid-winter you may see 15 or more species in a visit. The most abundant are usually teal or wigeon, though they may not be the easiest to see as teal often feed in marginal cover and wigeon fly out in flocks to feed on grassland and winter cereals. Shoveler and a dozen or so pintail are usually here until the turn of the year, whereas goldeneye and goosander mostly stay from November to February. In both spring and autumn there is a fair chance of garganey. The usual waterfowl exodus occurs about the end of March but then the influx of summer migrants begins. Eight or nine species of warbler breed in the plantations and the admirably extensive stands of scrub and tall herbage. Swifts and hirundines feed over the water and are hunted in turn by hobby. In fact Pitsford is notably good for raptor sightings. Sparrowhawk and kestrel are regular: marsh harrier, osprey, common buzzard, peregrine and merlin are recorded virtually every year. From September on, drawdown creates increasingly extensive areas of mudflats and shallowing pools within the reserve. This is ideal to pull in waders which are migrating south and the year's list usually extends to over 25 species including wood sandpiper, spotted redshank and whimbrel.

South of the causeway is much more disturbed by recreational uses but, as is so often the case, the deep water area approaching the dam is favoured by wintering divers, grebes and goosander so, at least on days when there is no sailing, it is worth allowing time to drop in at one of the two car parks at the western end of the reservoir and glance over the water.

Species	Mar-April	May-June	July-Oct	Nov-Feb
Gt. Crested Grebe	••••	••••	••••	••••
Little Grebe	••••	••••	••••	••••
Cormorant	•••		••	•••
Grey Heron	••••	••••	••••	••••
Mallard	••••	••••	••••	••••
Teal	••••	•	•••	••••
Garganey	•		•	
Gadwall	••••	••••	••••	••••
Wigeon	••••	•	•••	••••
Pintail	••••		••	••••
Shoveler	••••	•••	•••	•••
Tufted Duck	••••	••••	••••	••••
Pochard	••••	••••	••••	••••
Goldeneye	••••		•	••••
Ruddy Duck	••••	•••	••••	••••
Goosander	••••		•	••••
Smew				•
Shelduck	••		••	•
Greylag Goose	••••	••••	••••	••••
Canada Goose	••••	••••	••••	••••
Mute Swan	••••	••••	••••	••••
Sparrowhawk	••••	••••	••••	••••
Hobby		••	••	
Kestrel	•••	•••	•••	•••
Red-legged Partridge	••	••	••	••
Pheasant	••••	••••	••••	••••
Water Rail	•			•
Moorhen	••••	••••	••••	••••
Coot	••••	••••	••••	••••
Lapwing	••••	••	•••	••••
Ringed Plover			•••	••
Little Ringed Plover			••	
Golden Plover	••		••	•••
Snipe	••		•••	••••
Woodcock				••
Curlew			•	
Whimbrel		•	•	
Black-tailed Godwit			••	
Green Sandpiper			•••	•••
Wood Sandpiper			•	
Common Sandpiper	•••		••••	
Redshank	•••		•••	•••
Spotted Redshank			•••	
Greenshank	•		•••	
Little Stint			•	
Dunlin	•••		••••	••••
Ruff			••	
Gt Black-backed Gull	•		•	•••
Lesser "	•••		•••	••
Herring Gull	••	•	••	•
Common Gull	••••		•••	••••
Little Gull			•	
Black-headed Gull	••••	••	••••	••••
Black Tern		•		
Common Tern	•	••	••	
Arctic Tern	•		••	

68

Pitsford Birdwatching Calendar

Species				
Stock Dove	••••	••••	••••	••••
Woodpigeon	••••	••••	••••	••••
Turtle Dove			••	•••
Collared Dove	••••	••••	••••	••••
Cuckoo	••	••••	•	
Little Owl	•	•	•	•
Tawny Owl	•••	•••	•••	•••
Swift		••••	••	
Green Woodpecker	•••	•••	•••	••••
Great Spotted "	•••	•••	•••	•••
Swallow	••	••••	••••	
House Martin	•	••••	••••	
Sand Martin	••	••••	••	
Carrion Crow	••••	••••	••••	••••
Rook	••••	••••	••••	••••
Jackdaw	•••	•••	•••	•••
Magpie	••••	••••	••••	••••
Jay	•••	•••	••••	••••
Great Tit	••••	••••	••••	••••
Blue Tit	••••	••••	••••	••••
Coal Tit	••••	••••	••••	••••
Marsh Tit	••••	••••	••••	••••
Willow Tit	••••	••••	••••	••••
Long-tailed Tit	••••	••••	••••	••••
Nuthatch				•
Treecreeper	••••	••••	••••	••••
Wren	••••	••••	••••	••••
Mistle Thrush	••	••	••	••
Fieldfare	•••		•	••••
Song Thrush	••••	••••	••••	••••
Redwing	••			••••
Blackbird	••••	••••	••••	••••
Wheatear	••		•	
Robin	••••	••••	••••	••••
Grasshopper Warbler		••	••	
Reed Warbler		••	••	
Sedge Warbler		•••	•••	
Blackcap	•	••••	••••	
Garden Warbler	•	••••	••	
Whitethroat	•	••••	••	
Lesser Whitethroat	•	••••	••	
Willow Warbler	••	••••	••••	
Chiffchaff	••	••••	••••	
Goldcrest	•••	•••	•••	••••
Spotted Flycatcher		•••	•	
Dunnock	••••	••••	••••	••••
Meadow Pipit	•••		••	••••
Tree Pipit	•		•	
Pied Wagtail	••••	••••	••••	••••
Grey Wagtail	•		••	••
Yellow Wagtail	•	••••	•••	
Starling	••••	••••	••••	••••
Greenfinch	••••	••••	••••	••••
Goldfinch	••••	••••	••••	••••
Linnet	••••	••••	••••	••••
Redpoll	•	•	•••	•••
Bullfinch	••••	••••	••••	••••
Chaffinch	••••	••••	••••	••••

Species				
Brambling	•			•
Corn Bunting	••••	••••	••••	••••
Yellowhammer	••••	••••	••••	••••
Reed Bunting	••••	••••	••••	••••
House Sparrow	••••	••••	••••	••••
Tree Sparrow	••••	••••	••••	•••

Recent rarities include:- Black-throated Diver, Little Egret, Spoonbill, Velvet Scoter, Iceland Gull, Snow Bunting

Key: •••• Normally present/more than 90% of time
••• Frequently present/50%-90% of time
•• Less common/10-50% of time
• Scarce/less than 10% of time but not a rarity

69

Ravensthorpe Reservoir

Ravensthorpe Reservoir, is a very attractive reservoir. It is situated just off the M1 motorway, within easy reach of Northampton, Leicester and Coventry.

The reservoir dates back to 1890 and the water treatment works, located below the dam, is one of the oldest in the Anglian region. The Victorian building has recently been refurbished inside and out, using modern materials to restore and maintain the splendour of the Victorian architecture.

Ravensthorpe has a capacity of 1,882,000 cubic metres and supplies (together with Hollowell reservoir) 18,000 cubic metres of water per day. This forms part of the Ruthamford water supply network which supplies customers over an area of some 4,000 square kilometres.

Ravensthorpe Reservoir

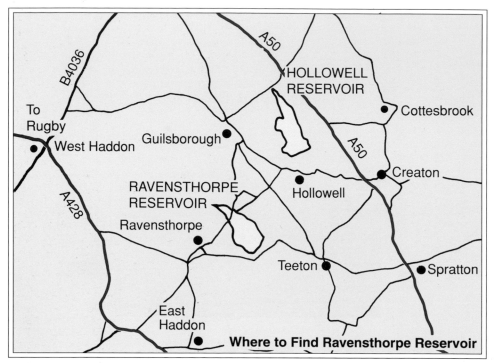

Where to Find Ravensthorpe Reservoir

Access from the M1 is at Junction 18 at Crick and through West Haddon on the A428 before turning left for Ravensthorpe village. The reservoir is situated beyond the village. Car parking is available near the reservoir dam on the road from Ravensthorpe village towards Teeton, as well as on the northern shore just over the causeway from the village on the right hand side. This scenic tranquil reservoir is an idyllic spot to relax and have a picnic.

Spanning 46 hectares Ravensthorpe supports an excellent trout fishery, some pike fishing is also available. The reservoir is stocked with big rainbow and brown trout throughout the season. Record rainbow trout exceeding 12 lbs were caught last season. Boat fishing courses are available, costs include fishing. To obtain day and evening permits or hire a boat visit the fishing lodge at the western side of the dam, tel. (0604) 770875. If you have enjoyed your visit to Ravensthorpe why not visit Hollowell Reservoir (a 5 minute drive) or Pitsford Water (about 10 minutes drive) which are close by? Birdwatching permits are available from the Pitsford Fishing Lodge.

Birdwatching at Ravensthorpe

Despite its small size, Ravensthorpe has recently been Anglian Water's best site for wintering little grebe, with over 40 present in some months plus breeding birds in summer. Admittedly this is not a species "rated" by most birders as it fails all four of the critical tests - it is not rare, it does not occur in enormous flocks, it is not at all that difficult to identify and it is not a bird of prey. We did change its name from dabchick in the hope of making it into a more worthwhile, serious bird but it didn't make much difference. On the other hand, if you're the sort of birdwatcher who just enjoys birds anyway, the dabchick is for you - plump, fluffy and slightly ridiculous in winter, sleek, smart and aggravatingly secretive in summer. Fringed by trees and a few small plantations Ravensthorpe has a good representative breeding bird assemblage including reed and sedge warbler, blackcap and chiffchaff and is frequently visited by green and greater spotted woodpeckers. Passage wader numbers are small but 9 or 10 species are recorded. Similarly, winter wildfowl rarely total over 400 birds but usually include about 10 species.

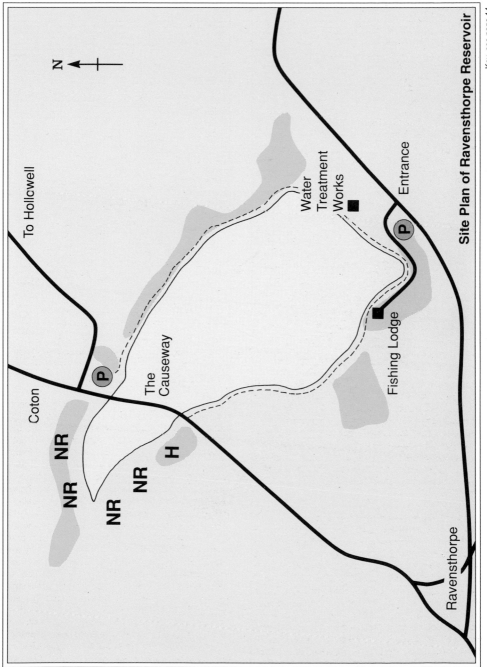

Site Plan of Ravensthorpe Reservoir

Key, see page 14

Ravensthorpe Birdwatching Calendar

Species	Mar-April	May-June	July-Oct	Nov-Feb
Gt. Crested Grebe	••••	••••	••••	••••
Little Grebe	••••	••••	••••	••••
Grey Heron	••••	•••	•••	•••
Mallard	••••	••••	••••	••••
Teal	••••			••••
Gadwall	••	•	•	••
Wigeon	•••			•••
Pintail	•			•
Shoveler	••			••
Tufted Duck	••••	••••	••••	••••
Pochard	••••		•	••••
Goldeneye	•••			••••
Ruddy Duck	••••	•••	•••	••••
Greylag Goose	••••	•••	•••	••••
Canada Goose	••••	••••	••••	••••
Mute Swan	•••	•••	•••	•••
Sparrowhawk	••	••	••	••
Kestrel	••	••	••	••
Red-legged Partridge	•	•	•	•
Pheasant	••	••	••	••
Water Rail	•			•
Moorhen	••••	••••	••••	••••
Coot	••••	••••	••••	••••
Lapwing	••		••	•••
Ringed Plover			•	
Little Ringed Plover			•	
Golden Plover			•	•
Snipe	•••		•••	•••
Green Sandpiper			•	
Common Sandpiper	••		•••	
Redshank			•	
Greenshank			•	
Dunlin			•	
Ruff			•	
Gt Black-backed Gull				•
Lesser "	••		••	••
Herring Gull			••	
Common Gull	••		••	••••
Black-headed Gull	••••		•••	••••
Common Tern	••		••	
Stock Dove	•••	•••	•••	•••
Woodpigeon	••••	••••	••••	••••
Turtle Dove		••	•	
Collard Dove	•••	•••	•••	•••
Cuckoo	•	•••	•	
Tawny Owl	•••	•••	•••	•••
Swift		••••	•••	
Green Woodpecker	•••	•••	•••	•••
Great Spotted "	•••	•••	•••	•••
Swallow		••••	••••	
House Martin		••••	••••	
Sand Martin	•	••	••	
Carrion Crow	••••	••••	••••	••••
Rook	••••	••••	••••	••••
Jackdaw	•••	•••	•••	•••
Magpie	•••	•••	•••	•••

Species	Mar-April	May-June	July-Oct	Nov-Feb
Jay	••			••
Great Tit	••••	••••	••••	••••
Blue Tit	••••	••••	••••	••••
Coal Tit	••••	••••	••••	••••
Marsh Tit	••••	••••	••••	••••
Willow Tit	••	••	••	••
Long-tailed Tit	•••	•••	•••	•••
Treecreeper	•••	•••	•••	•••
Wren	••••	••••	••••	••••
Mistle Thrush	••••	••••	••••	••••
Fieldfare	••			•••
Song Thrush	••••	••••	••••	••••
Redwing	••			•••
Blackbird	••••	••••	••••	••••
Robin	••••	••••	••••	••••
Reed Warbler		••••	••••	
Sedge Warbler		••••	••••	
Blackcap	•••	••••	••••	
Garden Warbler		••	••	
Whitethroat		••	••	
Lesser Whitethroat		••	••	
Willow Warbler	•••	••••	••••	
Chiffchaff	•••	••••	••••	
Goldcrest	•••	•••	•••	•••
Spotted Flycatcher		•••	•••	
Dunnock	••••	••••	••••	••••
Meadow Pipit				••
Pied Wagtail	••••	••••	••••	••••
Grey Wagtail	•			•
Yellow Wagtail	••	••	••	
Starling	••••	••••	••••	••••
Greenfinch	••••	••••	••••	••••
Goldfinch	•••	•••	•••	•••
Linnet	••	•	••	••
Redpoll	••			••
Bullfinch	••	••	••	••
Chaffinch	••••	••••	••••	••••
Brambling	•			•
Yellowhammer	••••	••	•••	••••
Reed Bunting	••••	••••	••••	••••
House Sparrow	••••	••••	••••	••••
Tree Sparrow	••	•	•	••

Recent rarities include:- Black-necked Grebe, Whimbrel, Wood Sandpiper, Hen Harrier, Mediterranean Gull

Key: ••••   Normally present/more than 90% of time
   •••   Frequently present/50%-90% of time
   ••   Less common/10-50% of time
   •   Scarce/less than 10% of time but not a rarity

Rutland Reservoir

Rutland Water is situated near Oakham in the old county of Rutland. It is Anglian's largest reservoir.

It was completed in 1977 and covers 1,250 hectares. Water is pumped into the reservoir from the River Nene at Wansford and the River Welland at Tinwell. After storage in the reservoir it is then treated and processed at Wing water treatment works.

Rutland Water

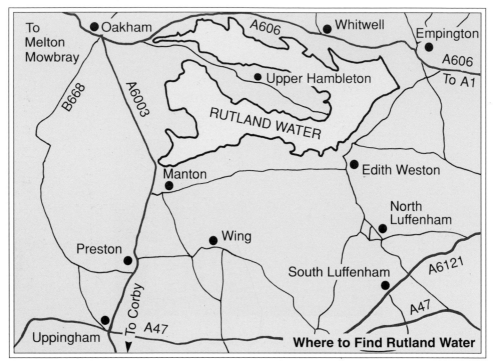

To Melton Mowbray • Oakham — A606 — • Whitwell — Empington • — A606 — To A1 — • Upper Hambleton — RUTLAND WATER — B668 — A6003 — Manton • — • Edith Weston — North Luffenham • — • Wing — Preston • — South Luffenham • — A6121 — To Corby — A47 — Uppingham • — A47

Where to Find Rutland Water

Rutland Water can be found less than 10 minutes drive west of the A1 near Stamford. Follow the A606 towards Oakham. You will find routes to the north and south shores of the reservoir are well signposted. If you are travelling from the west take the A47 (from Leicester) then A6003 towards Oakham and follow the signs to the reservoir. There is ample car parking at the four main car parks (Barnsdale, Whitwell and Sykes Lane on the north shore, and Normanton on the south shore). All have toilets and refreshments. You will also find two adventure playgrounds for children under 13 years of age. These are located at Sykes Lane and Barnsdale car parks.

The reservoir's storage capacity of 124,000,000 cubic metres provides water for domestic and industrial consumption as part of the strategic Ruthamford water supply network. This covers an area of 4,000 square kilometres and includes the towns of Peterborough, Northampton, Milton Keynes, Bedford, Kettering, Corby and Wellingborough. The name of the system is derived from the names of the three largest

reservoirs; Rutland, Grafham and Pitsford. While Rutland plays a vital role in the Ruthamford supply network, it is also well established as a water sports and leisure centre of international repute. The thriving Rutland Sailing Club (RSC) occupies a club house and stretch of shoreline at Edith Weston and attracts yachtsmen and dinghy sailors from all over the country. A well-equipped Residential Centre at the club provides excellent accommodation and teaching facilities for groups coming to Rutland specially for instruction in sailing, fishing or any other activity associated with the reservoir. For further details contact the Secretary, Rutland Sailing Club, Gibbet Lane, Edith Weston, near Stamford, Rutland LE15 8HL. Tel. Stamford (0780) 720292 (except Tuesdays and Wednesdays). For non-RSC members there is day sailing available at the Whitwell Sailing Centre on the Whitwell Creek. The centre is open all year and is fully equipped with changing rooms, showers and toilets. Dinghies can be parked at Whitwell for overnight, week or seasonal periods provided you obtain a permit from the centre. Devotees of the newer and increasingly popular sport of

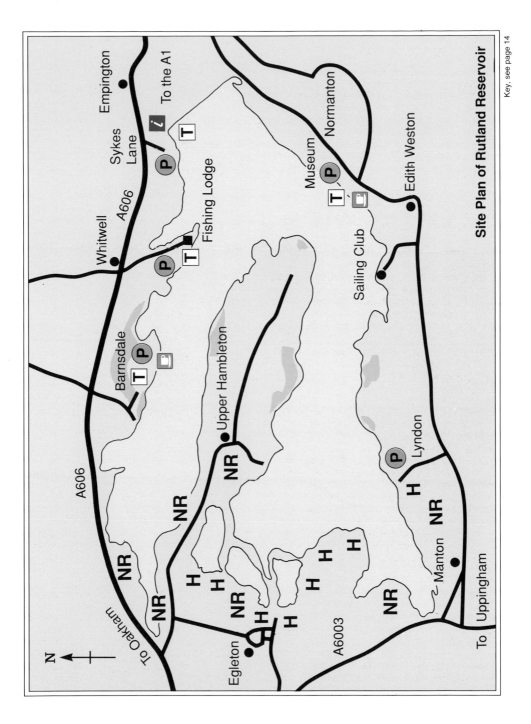

Site Plan of Rutland Reservoir

Key, see page 14

windsurfing also have their base at Whitwell Creek. A sailboard school operates from the Sailing Centre and tuition is available. You can hire or buy sailboards and wetsuits from the Centre. For more information on day sailing and windsurfing tel. (078086) 464. If sailing and windsurfing sound a bit energetic then why not take a leisurely trip on the Rutland Belle? This comfortable passenger cruiser offers you the opportunity to tour the giant reservoir and appreciate views usually enjoyed only by anglers and sailors. There is room for 75 passengers on the main deck and another 36 on the upper sun deck. Regular tour services operate each day from Whitwell during the season. Charter by groups is available. For details of services please ring Rutland Water Cruises Limited on (057284) 630.

Keen anglers will know Rutland Water enjoys the reputation for being one of the finest fisheries in Europe. Combine its excellent trout stocks with superb facilities and you have a location for national and international competitions. The reservoir offers top quality trout fishing with a good chance of really big fish. Rainbow and brown trout over 12 lbs have been caught at Rutland. If you need some tips or instruction there are courses and individual tuition for beginners as well as the more experienced angler. Call at the Fishing Lodge in Whitwell Creek. The Lodge offers excellent facilities for club events and competitions. You can also obtain permits there and book one of the fleet of 66 powered boats. Whitwell Fishing Lodge, Whitwell, Oakham, Leics LE15 8BW, Tel. (078086) 770.

Walkers and cyclists are well catered for at Rutland. The 42 kilometre waterside cycle track passes all the main points of interest and includes the beautiful Hambleton peninsula. Cycles of all types for all ages can be hired from either Whitwell or Normanton. The cycles include tricycles with childrens seats and most have baskets for picnics. For further information, bookings or a free leaflet please telephone either Whitwell (078086) 705 or Normanton (0780) 720888. The Nature Reserve at the western end of the reservoir offers walkers the chance to combine a pleasant walk with an hour or two birdwatching. The reserve covers 146 hectares and visitors are welcome at both sections, Lyndon Hill and Egleton.

If you prefer a more leisurely stroll then why not explore Barnsdale Drought Garden on the north shore. It was recently created to show the wide

Species	Mar-April	May-June	July-Oct	Nov-Feb
Gt. Crested Grebe	••••	••••	••••	••••
Red-necked Grebe			••	••
Slavonian Grebe			•	•
Black-necked Grebe	•		•••	
Little Grebe	••••	••••	••••	••••
Cormorant	••••	••••	••••	••••
Grey Heron	••••	••••	••••	••••
Mallard	••••	••••	••••	••••
Teal	••••	••••	••••	••••
Garganey		•	••	
Gadwall	••••	••••	••••	••••
Wigeon	••••	••••	••••	••••
Pintail	••••	••	••••	••••
Shoveler	••••	••••	••••	••••
Tufted Duck	••••	••••	••••	••••
Pochard	••••	••••	••••	••••
Scaup	••			•••
Goldeneye	••••	••	••	••••
Ruddy Duck	••••	••••	••••	••••
Red-breasted Merganser				••
Goosander				••••
Smew				••••
Shelduck	••••	••••	••••	••••
White-fronted Goose				•
Greylag Goose	••••	••••		••••
Pink footed Goose				•
Canada Goose	••••	••••	••••	••••
Egyptian Goose	••••	••••	••••	••••
Mute Swan	••••	••••	••••	••••
Bewick's Swan			••	••
Sparrowhawk	••••	••••	••••	•••
Osprey	•	•	•	
Hobby	•	••	••	
Kestrel	••••	••••	••••	••••
Red-legged Partridge	•	•	•	•
Pheasant	••••	••••	••••	••••
Water Rail			•••	•••
Moorhen	••••	••••	••••	••••
Coot	••••	••••	••••	••••
Oystercatcher	••••	••••	•	
Lapwing	••••	••••	••••	••••
Ringed Plover	••	•••	••	
Little Ringed Plover	••	••	•	
Golden Plover			••	••••
Snipe	••••	•••	••••	••••
Jack Snipe	•		••	••
Woodcock	••••	••••	••••	••••
Curlew	•••	•	•	••
Whimbrel	•	•	•	
Black-tailed Godwit	•		•	
Green Sandpiper	•	••	••••	••••
Wood Sandpiper			•	
Common Sandpiper	•		••••	
Redshank	••••	•••	••••	•••
Spotted Redshank			••••	
Greenshank	•	•	••••	

Rutland Water Birdwatching Calendar

Species					Species				
Little Stint			••		Willow Warbler	••••	••••	••••	
Dunlin	••••	•	•••	••••	Chiffchaff	••••	••••	••••	•
Ruff	••	•	••••	••••	Goldcrest	••••	••••	••••	••••
Turnstone			•		Spotted Flycatcher		••••	••••	
Gt Black-backed Gull	••••	••••	••••	••••	Dunnock	••••	••••	••••	••••
Lesser "	••		••••	•	Wren	••••	••••	••••	••••
Herring Gull	•		••••	••••	Meadow Pipit	•••	••••	•	••••
Common Gull	••••	••••	••••	••••	Tree Pipit		•		
Little Gull	••	•	••••		Pied Wagtail	••••	••••	••••	••••
Black-headed Gull	••••	••••	••••	••••	Grey Wagtail				•••
Black Tern	•	•	•••		Yellow Wagtail	•••	••••	•••	
Common Tern	•••	••••	••••		Starling	••••	••••	••••	••••
Arctic Tern	•••	••	•		Greenfinch	••••	••••	••••	••••
Stock Dove	••••	••••	••••	••••	Goldfinch	••••	••••	••••	•••
Woodpigeon	••••	••••	••••	••••	Linnet	••••	••••	••••	••••
Turtle Dove		••••	•••		Redpoll	••••	••••	••••	••••
Collard Dove	••••	••••	••••	••••	Bullfinch	••••	••••	••••	••••
Cuckoo	•••	••••	•••		Chaffinch	••••	••••	••••	••••
Little Owl	•	•	•	•	Drambling				•••
Tawny Owl	••••	/ ••••	••••	••••	Yellowhammer	••••	••••	••••	••••
Swift	••	••••	••••		Reed Bunting	••••	••••	••••	••••
Green Woodpecker	••••	••••	••••	••••	House Sparrow	••••	••••	••••	••••
Gt Spotted "	••••	••••	••••	••••	Tree Sparrow	••••	••••	••••	••••
Lesser Spotted "	••••	••••	••••	••••					
Skylark	••••	••••	••••	••••					
Swallow	•••	••••	••••						
House Martin	•••	••••	••••						
Sand Martin	••••	••••	••••						
Carrion Crow	••••	••••	••••	••••					
Rook	••••	••••	••••	••••					
Jackdaw	••••	••••	••••	••••					
Magpie	••••	••••	••••	••••					
Jay	••••	••••	••••	••••					
Great Tit	••••	••••	••••	••••					
Blue Tit	••••	••••	••••	••••					
Coal Tit	••••	••••	••••	••••					
Marsh Tit	••••	••••	••••	••••					
Willow Tit	••••	••••	••••	••••					
Long-tailed Tit	••••	••••	••••	••••					
Nuthatch	••••	••••	••••	••••					
Treecreeper	••••	••••	••••	••••					
Mistle Thrush	••••	••••	••••	••••					
Fieldfare	•••		•	••••					
Song Thrush	••••	••••	••••	••••					
Redwing	•••		•	••••					
Blackbird	••••	••••	••••	••••					
Wheatear	••		•						
Nightingale	•••	••••							
Redstart	•		•						
Robin	••••	••••	••••	••••					
Whinchat	•		•						
Grasshopper Warbler	••••	••••	••••						
Reed Warbler		••••	••••						
Sedge Warbler	••••	••••	••••						
Blackcap	••••	••••	••••	•					
Garden Warbler	••••	••••	••••						
Whitethroat	••••	••••	••••						
Lesser Whitethroat	••••	••••	••••						

Recent rarities include:- Caspian Tern, Ring-necked Duck, Green-winged Teal, White-winged Black Tern, Great White Egret

Key: •••• Normally present/more than 90% of time
••• Frequently present/50%-90% of time
•• Less common/10-50% of time
• Scarce/less than 10% of time but not a rarity

variety of plants and shrubs which can grow in the British climate without extra watering. TV gardener, Geoff Hamilton, presenter of BBC's Gardeners' World and a Rutland local, helped create the garden which incorporates a variety of techniques for moisture retention. Next to the Drought Garden you will find the Arboretum, planted with the twenty one tree species used in Anglian Water's extensive planting programme. Follow the waymarked route and see how many you can spot. Rutland Water was originally landscaped by Dame Sylvia Crowe. She was commissioned to ensure it blended as naturally as possible into the Rutland environment.

On your travels around Rutland you cannot miss Normanton Church, stood on its own peninsula overlooking the reservoir. The original church was part of the Normanton manor estate which belonged to the Umfraville family in medieval times. The estate was bought in 1729 by Sir Gilbert Heathcote, the first baronet. The medieval church was demolished in 1764 and replaced by a small plain building. In 1862 most of the present church was built in the same style as St Johns in Smiths

Square, Westminster, London, with the nave and chancel completed in 1911. When plans for the reservoir were approved, the church was deconsecrated, the burial vault emptied, and monuments to the Heathcote family removed. Yet this well-known landmark might have been lost in the 1970's as it would have become submerged once the reservoir was filled. Rather than demolish it or try to move it stone by stone and erect it above the water line, efforts were made to preserve it. The foundations were reinforced with concrete and the church surrounded with an embankment. The floor level was raised and the masonry proofed against damp. Today you can visit the church which houses a fascinating museum. It is open daily throughout the season from 1st April to end of September (11.00 am - 5.00 pm) Winter season, Sunday only. For further information about all that Rutland Water and the surrounding area has to offer call in at the Tourist Information Centre at Sykes Lane car park.

Birdwatching at Rutland Water

Rutland Water is one of the best places in Britain to see waterfowl. In winter there are usually over 10,000 birds of about 20 different species present. In spring and autumn the reservoir attracts exceptional numbers of migrating waders and on several occasions 19 species have been seen on a single day. In summer up to 12 species of wildfowl nest and large numbers arrive to moult as soon as breeding is over. There is an impressive list of rare birds which have been recorded here. The site is very large and many species are best seen by going to the nature reserves which extend for nine miles along the western shores. Two parts of the reserves are open to the public. Both have well-sited hides which give good, close-up views of birds. One hide in each part is designed for wheelchair users.

Lyndon Reserve is planned for families and newcomers to the wildlife of Rutland Water. There is a visitor centre and the Gibbet Gorse nature trail which winds through a variety of habitats including woodlands and scrub. There are also several ponds full of aquatic life. These areas are at their best in spring and summer when there is lots of birdsong, butterflies on the wing and frogs and newts active in the ponds. There are also hides overlooking the water; the main waterfowl interest present in autumn and winter. Allow an hour or two for a leisurely visit. The Lyndon Reserve is reached following signs for 'Rutland Water Southern Shore'.

The road to the reserve is off the road from Edith Weston to Manton. In winter it is open only at weekends. From Good Friday to the end of October it is also open on Tuesday, Wednesday and Thursday. Opening times are 10.00am to 4.00pm.

Egleton Reserve is excellent both for beginners and experienced birdwatchers. Its three lagoons hold water even when the reservoir is drawn down, attracting a remarkable variety of wildfowl and waders which can be seen easily from the eleven hides. There are also opportunities to watch birds in grassland, scrub and woodland. It's easy to spend two or three hours at this site, or all day. The Egleton Reserve is reached via Egleton village. Follow signs from the southernmost corner of the village. It is open year round on Wednesdays, Fridays, Saturdays and Sundays, and at Bank Holidays, from 9.00am to 4.00pm. Both reserves are manned, so you can get advice on what birds are about on the day of your visit.

Away from the reserves there are plenty of other rewarding sites. The Normanton car park gives excellent visibility over a large area of open water and it is worth walking eastward from here towards the dam for wintering divers and sea duck which favour the deep open water here. The dam itself can also be traversed from the Sykes Lane car park. In stormy conditions, birds may shelter in the bays along the north shore. The one near Barnsdale car park is best viewed from the hide midway along the woodland nature trail which runs east from here toward Whitwell car park. This trail passes through broadleaved woodland and a small conifer plantation. The area is visited by all three woodpeckers and woodcock while in spring and summer it attracts a good variety of songbirds including warblers and nightingales. By driving to the end of the Hambleton peninsula and parking off the road you can make a circular walk of about 5 miles (plus optional pub stop!) through varied countryside and woodland with good views over both arms of Rutland Water and the ever-present chance of new species to add to your day's list!

Willen Lake

Willen Lake lies on the north-east outskirts of Milton Keynes surrounded by 24 hectares of attractive parkland. The reservoir serves a vital function as one of the city's balancing lakes. These lakes are designed to hold, temporarily, the vast quantities of rainwater which pours off rooftops and roads into the drains and rivers, and so prevent flooding of towns and villages downstream of Milton Keynes.

Besides helping control floodwater, Willen Lake provides an excellent area for recreation which is permanently accessible. The lake is divided into two basins and both are skirted by hard surfaced paths which are suitable for pedestrians, joggers and cyclists alike. The north basin, with its distinctive island, is a peaceful place reserved for wildfowl.

Willen Lake

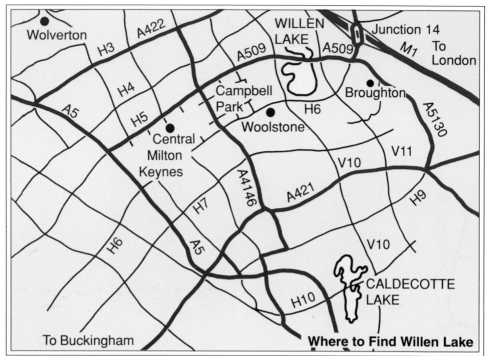

Wolverton

H3

A422

A509

WILLEN LAKE

A509

Junction 14

M_1

To London

H4

Campbell Park

H6

Broughton

A5130

A5

H5

Woolstone

Central Milton Keynes

V10

V11

A4146

A421

H9

H7

H6

A5

V10

CALDECOTTE LAKE

H10

To Buckingham

Where to Find Willen Lake

Willen Lake is situated only 3 kilometres from junction 14 of the M1 motorway. Follow the A509 and then Childs Way (H6), which takes you around the south lake. Turn right along Brickhill Street (V10) and follow the signs for the lake car parks and water sports. Alternatively, if you come into Milton Keynes on the A6 pick up the A509 and follow Portway (H6) until you reach the Pagoda roundabout where you either turn left along Brickhill Street and park near the Peace Pagoda to enjoy the view over the north basin, or you turn right along Brickhill Street and follow sign for lakeside parking and water sports on the south basin. There is ample car parking and it is free!

The River Ouzel once flowed through the middle of what is now Willen Lake but it was diverted round the lake during the lake excavations. This explains why the river has the appearance of a canal at this point. Look out for the masses of small white flowers which cover the river in the summer. These blooms are River or Water Crowfoot - notice they are similar to those of the buttercup to which they are related. The embankment between the lake

and the river prevents floodwater entering the lake except via weir gates. The weir gates are part of a floodwater control system controlled by a central computer. A massive gate, usually submerged under the river, can be raised or lowered, impounding or releasing floodwater. Impounded water can be diverted into the lake and held there until the swollen river subsides and the excess water can be discharged back into it gradually.

As you walk or cycle around the north basin you cannot miss the Peace Pagoda, the white oriental building set on the hillside overlooking the lake. It was the first Peace Pagoda to be built in Europe by the Nipponzan Myohoji sect, and it enshrines ancient sacred relics of Lord Buddha. The monks say it represents a symbolic focus of peace and brotherhood. The Pagoda is at its most beautiful in the Spring set against a thousand cherry trees which grow on the surrounding hillside. They were planted in remembrance of the victims of all wars and were donated by the ancient Japanese town of Yoshino, famous for the beauty of the cherry blossom. After its dedication in September 1980,

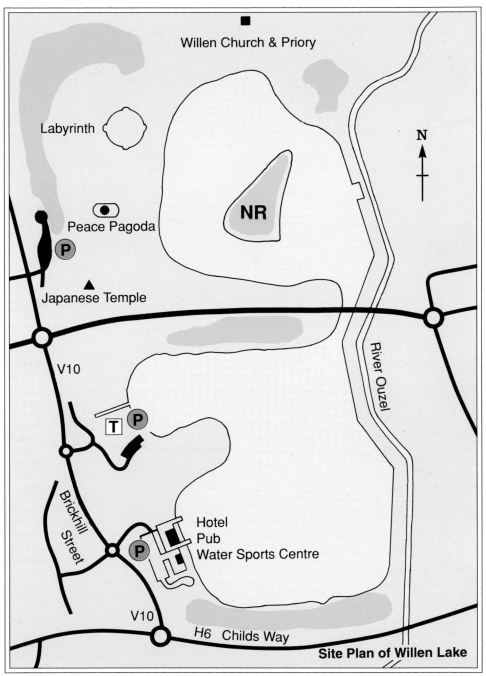

Willen Church & Priory

Labyrinth

NR

N

Peace Pagoda

P

Japanese Temple

V10

River Ouzel

T P

Brickhill Street

Hotel
Pub
Water Sports Centre

P

V10

H6 Childs Way

Site Plan of Willen Lake

Key, see page 14

83

several monks stayed on to maintain the Pagoda and they would be very pleased to welcome you at the temple nearby. You may also wish to visit Willen Church and Priory situated on the north lake. Willen Church, St Mary Magdalene, is largely of late 17th century date, being built about 1680 by Dr Richard Busby at a total cost of £5,000 - a very large sum indeed for that period! It was designed by Robert Hooke, a contemporary of Sir Christopher Wren. Notice the unusual carved pineapples which crown the tower and front porch. The tower contains three bells from the chandlers foundry at Drayton Parslow 1683. Brothers of the Order of the Society of the Sacred Mission run the church and priory.

The 100 acre south basin bustles with a wide variety of water sports and other leisure activities. At the Water Sports Centre you can try windsurfing, dinghy sailing or canoeing. Expert tutors offer a range of courses which cater both for adults and juniors. Alternatively, why not hire a rowing boat in the north bay of the south lake or hire one of a variety of cycles (childs, sports, shoppers, mountain) from the Water Sports Centre and explore the "Redway" cycle system which runs throughout Milton Keynes. Maps are available along with pumps, repair kits and locks. Bikes can be hired for up to 3 hours, all day, even weekly and may be booked in advance.

For further details of courses and hire rates please enquire at the Centre or ring (0908) 670197.

For those who prefer riding horses there is a bridleway along the east shore of the south basin which crosses the channel and passes along the south shore of the north lake - just follow the signs.

If you want a more leisurely time there are a couple of picnic areas overlooking the south lake. Within the parkland there you will find an excellent children's adventure playground and an Italian ice cream parlour. If you want a meal try the "Shorebreak" cafe which provides food for a wide range of tastes, or takeaway snacks are available from the servery in the Centre. The Wayfarers Hotel provides good bar meals and you will find a family area in the bar or you could try their restaurant.

Birdwatching at Willen Lake

Whatever your level of interest in birds, Willen Lake is well worth visiting. Despite its location, surrounded by the city of Milton Keynes, it attracts a very good range of birds at all times of year, with over 190 species recorded since its creation in 1974. It also has a large community of free-loaders in the form of mallard, geese and mute swans which march up to you and demand to be fed! Mostly these birds frequent the southern basin which is uninhabitable for many of the shyer species because it is heavily disturbed by recreational uses.

The main ornithological interest is on the northern basin, with its large island, or in the surrounding areas of grassland, trees and shrubs.

Total wildfowl numbers from September to February are about the 1000 mark and can rise to over 1500. These are mostly the common species but they often include over 100 teal, similar numbers of shoveler and a substantial flock of wigeon. Several species remain to breed, with mallard, gadwall, shoveler and tufted duck resting on the island which also has a colony of common terns. Greylag and Canada geese are very numerous all year – most birdwatchers regard them with disdain because they are introduced birds but the flocks are fine spectacle to the open-minded!

There is a very varied songbird community especially in summer when resident thrushes, tits and finches are augmented by at least six species of warbler, spotted flycatcher and yellow wagtail.

The number and variety of waders vary depending on water levels but usually over 20 species are recorded in both spring and autumn passage.

Taken overall, this is the best birdwatching site in Buckinghamshire. Compared with many reservoirs, the north basin is small and easily accessible from the car parks and the footpath network so that you can make a worthwhile visit in your lunch break if you work nearby or spend two or three hours looking round the site more thoroughly.

Willen Lake Birdwatching Calendar

Species	Mar-April	May-June	July-Oct	Nov-Feb
Gt. Crested Grebe	••••	••••	••••	••••
Little Grebe	••	••	•••	••
Cormorant	•••	•	•••	••••
Grey Heron	••••	•••	••••	••••
Mallard	••••	••••	••••	••••
Teal	••••	•	••••	••••
Gadwall	••••	••••	••••	••••
Wigeon	•••	•	•••	••••
Pintail				•
Shoveler	••••	•••	••••	••••
Tufted Duck	••••	••••	••••	••••
Pochard	••••	••	••••	••••
Goldeneye	•••		•	••••
Ruddy Duck	•	•	•	•
Goosander				•
Shelduck	•••	•••	•••	•••
Greylag Goose	••••	••••	••••	••••
Canada Goose	••••	••••	••••	••••
Mute Swan	••••	••••	••••	••••
Sparrowhawk	••	•	••	••
Hobby		•	•	
Kestrel	•••	•••	•••	•••
Water Rail	•			•
Moorhen	••••	••••	••••	••••
Coot	••••	••••	••••	••••
Oystercatcher	•			
Lapwing	••••	••••	••••	••••
Ringed Plover	••••	••••	••••	
Little Ringed Plover	•••	••••	•••	
Golden Plover	•		•	•
Snipe	•••		•••	••••
Curlew	•			
Wimbrel	•	•	•	
Black-tailed Godwit	•	•	•	
Green Sandpiper	•	•	••	•
Common Sandpiper	••	•••	••••	
Redshank	••••	••••	••••	•
Spotted Redshank		•	••	
Greenshank	•	•	•••	
Little Stint		•	••	
Dunlin	•••	•	•••	••
Ruff	••	•	••	
Gt Black-backed Gull	••		•	•••
Lesser "	•••	•	•••	•••
Herring Gull	•••		••	•••
Common Gull	•••		•••	••••
Little Gull	•	•		
Black-headed Gull	••••	••••	••••	••••
Black Tern	•	••	•	
Common Tern	•••	••••	•••	
Arctic Tern	•	•		
Stock Dove	•••	•••	•••	•••
Woodpigeon	••••	••••	••••	••••
Turtle Dove		••	••	
Collared Dove	••••	••••	••••	••••
Cuckoo	••	••••	•	
Swift		••••	•••	

Species	Mar-April	May-June	July-Oct	Nov-Feb
Kingfisher	•••	•••	•••	•••
Green Woodpecker	•	•	•	•
Gt Spotted "	•	•	•	•
Skylark	••••	••••	••••	••••
Swallow	••	••••	•••	
House Martin	••	••••	•••	
Sand Martin	•••	••••	•••	
Carrion Crow	••••	••••	••••	••••
Rook	••••	••••	••••	••••
Jackdaw	••••	••••	••••	••••
Magpie	••••	••••	••••	••••
Great Tit	••••	••••	••••	••••
Blue Tit	••••	••••	••••	••••
Long Tailed Tit	••••	••••	••••	••••
Wren	••••	••••	••••	••••
Mistle Thrush	••••	••••	••••	••••
Fieldfare	•		•	••••
Song Thrush	••••	••••	••••	••••
Rodwing	•		•	••••
Blackbird	••••	••••	••••	••••
Wheatear	••	•	•	••
Whinchat		•	•	
Robin	••••	••••	••••	••••
Grasshopper Warbler		•		
Reed Warbler		••••	••••	
Sedge Warbler	••	••••	•••	
Blackcap	••	••••	••••	
Garden Warbler		••••	•••	
Whitethroat	•	•••	•••	
Lesser Whitethroat		•••	•••	
Willow Warbler	••	••••	•••	
Chiffchaff	•••	••••	••••	
Goldcrest	•••		•••	••••
Spotted Flycatcher		•••	•••	
Dunnock	••••	••••	••••	••••
Meadow Pipit	••••	••••	••••	••••
Pied Wagtail	••••	••••	••••	••••
Grey Wagtail	•••		•••	•••
Yellow Wagtail	••	••••	•••	
Starling	••••	••••	••••	••••
Greenfinch	••••	••••	••••	••••
Goldfinch	••••	••••	••••	••••
Linnet	•••	•••	•••	•••
Redpoll	•	•	•	••
Siskin	•			••
Bullfinch	••••	••••	••••	••••
Chaffinch	••••	••••	••••	••••
Brambling				•
Corn Bunting	•	•	•	•
Yellowhammer	•••	•••	•••	•••
Reed Bunting	••••	••••	••••	•••
House Sparrow	••••	••••	••••	••••
Tree Sparrow	••••	••••	••••	••••

Recent rarities include:- Bittern, Avocet, Caspian Tern, Firecrest

Key: ••••   Normally present/more than 90% of time
   •••   Frequently present/50%-90% of time
   ••   Less common/10-50% of time
   •   Scarce/less than 10% of time but not a rarity

BIRDS

OF ANGLIAN WATER RESERVOIRS

Identification Guide

STARTING BIRD IDENTIFICATION

This section illustrates and describes the birds you are most likely to see on Anglian Water's reservoirs. If you've not tried to identify birds before, start with the ones which stick around for long enough to let you get a good look at them – Canada geese, mallard, moorhen and coot for example. These are birds which can easily be seen from the main car parks at each site. Knowing them confidently will help you to identify other species.

Some birds have very distinctive colouring – like shelducks – or shape, like herons. Others have characteristic ways of behaving – if it's a waterbird, does it dive like a coot or upend like a mallard? If it's on the shore, does it run like a wagtail or hop like a reed bunting? If it's in a tree is it acrobatic like a blue tit or upright like a robin? What a bird does and how it moves are always helpful in narrowing down its possible identity.

Other important clues are when you see it and where. Some birds are only present at one time of year. And most birds stick to particular habitats – woodland, grassy areas, muddy shores or open water, for example.

Even after the bird has flown or swum off, you can often put together all these pointers and confidently decide what it was. But not always – if it was too easy, it wouldn't be any fun. Good luck!

CORMORANT

IDENTIFICATION: Cormorants have a very distinctive shape. When swimming they look long and low with no visible tail and the beak is always held pointing slightly upwards. On land they often stand with wings half spread like heraldic laundry. In this posture, adults show a white patch on each thigh while young birds are almost completely white on throat and underparts.
FLIGHT: With neck stretched out and wings beating purposefully, the birds look slow but actually travel quite fast. They often form up in long lines or V-formation.
SEASON: Most present in autumn and winter but some stay all year.
VOICE: Gutteral croaks when squabbling or at nesting colonies.

HABITAT: Mostly large water bodies or perched on open shores, rafts or water towers.
FOOD: Fish of all kinds, usually caught at depths of 1-3m, but will dive to 9m.
NEST: A bulky stick structure. A few birds nest inland in waterside trees but most breed on rocky islands off the coast.

While most diving birds have plumage which keeps out water, cormorants' feathers allow it to penetrate. This reduces their buoyancy and means they can dive to pursue fish with less effort. The drawback is that they must then drip-dry themselves.

HERON

IDENTIFICATION: With its neck stretched out, the heron's tall angular shape is unmistakable. A resting bird can look quite different because it contrives to tuck in its neck and apparently hunches its shoulders so that it seems altogether more squat and plump. However, its pale blue-grey back, dagger-like beak and long legs still reveal its identity.
FLIGHT: The long neck is curved back, making the bird look very deep-chested. The feet project well beyond its tail and the wings are broad, rounded and down-curved.
SEASON: All year.
VOICE: A loud, harsh and irritable "fraank" which carries far over water.

HABITAT: Water margins and shallows, from large lakes to ditches and garden ponds.
FOOD: Fish especially eels, frogs, small birds and rodents – basically whatever comes in range and is small enough to swallow!
NEST: A bulky structure in treetops. The colony may be far from water in a wood and the same sites will be used for many years if undisturbed.

Herons are very vulnerable to cold weather when shallows freeze and fish stay deep. Weakened by hunger they may be easy to approach but disturbance means that their fishing fails and the birds waste vital energy when they fly off so do try to keep away from fishing herons especially in winter.

CORMORANT
Length: about 90cm

HERON
Length: about 95cm

GREAT CRESTED GREBE

IDENTIFICATION: Very streamlined and slim swimming and diving birds, much paler-coloured than any duck. Very distinctive in spring and summer with their handsome chestnut ruffs. In autumn, the ruff is moulted and birds have drab grey upperparts with a white throat and neck. Often swims with neck erect but can hunch its head right down. Chicks are striped black and white.
FLIGHT: Usually low over the water, the long neck and trailing feet giving a very "stretched" and slender appearance. Two white patches show up on the wing and birds always look pale overall.
SEASON: Large numbers in winter. Only a few pairs breed on reservoirs.
VOICE: Adults have a rasping bark "rah-rah-rah" and a far-carrying resonant growl.

HABITAT: Medium-sized and large waterbodies. Reservoirs often get a big winter influx when gravel pits freeze up.
FOOD: Small fish.
NEST: Floating platform of waterweed anchored amongst reeds or, sometimes, on a snag in the open.

Brought near to extinction in the last century when the headfeathers were collected to adorn ladies' hats! Adults have a delightful spring courtship display, "dancing" face to face while offering each other gifts of waterweed.

LITTLE GREBE

IDENTIFICATION: In winter, both adults are a dingy brown above with a fawn wedge running forward from the tail. They usually look fluffed up and seem to float high in the water like a toy. In spring and summer they are dark brown with a rich chestnut face and throat. The yellow spot on the base of the beak is often quite conspicuous.
FLIGHT: Rarely seen airborne by day.
SEASON: Mostly on reservoirs in winter and on reed-fringed pools, lakes and rivers in the breeding season.
VOICE: An unmistakable high-pitched whinnying.

HABITAT: Waters of all sizes but usually less than 1m deep so tending to be seen near the shore on reservoirs.
FOOD: Aquatic insects, snails, shrimps or reeds.
NEST: A floating platform of waterplants often anchored well offshore on a weedy pool or river.

Only half the size of most ducks, little grebes are easy to overlook even on small waters and they are usually shy of humans, diving promptly to swim underwater and re-surface amongst the cover of water plants, where they contrive to float low in the water and make themselves as inconspicuous as possible.

MALLARD

IDENTIFICATION: The commonest duck. Look for the green head, white collar and brown breast of males. Females are brown and can be confused with some other ducks but are a lot bigger than teal and lack the heavy-beaked appearance of shoveler. Female gadwall are very like them but mallard have a blue patch- the speculum - on the wing and gadwall have white. Fortunately females are often with males which makes their identity obvious. Some reservoirs have flocks of hybrid mallard - some white, some nearly black: dark birds with white breasts are quite common.
FLIGHT: Fast and direct – the blue speculum is often conspicuous.
SEASON: All year. Often with other kinds of ducks.
VOICE: The familiar loud quack is made only by the females.

HABITAT: Almost all water bodies, rivers, ponds and marshes, mostly congregating in sheltered, shallow waters.
FOOD: Waterplants, seeds, small snails, aquatic insects, shrimps, grain, bread and cake.
NEST: On ground in tall vegetation, or in hole or hollow tree often far from water. Sometimes in gardens.

Male mallard lose their bright, curly-tailed plumage in late summer and look much like the females until their breeding plumage reappears in autumn when pairs form ready for an early start with nesting in the spring.

GREAT CRESTED GREBE
Length: about 50cm

Chick

LITTLE GREBE
Length: about 26cm

Female

Male

MALLARD
Length: about 60cm

GADWALL

IDENTIFICATION: An easy duck to overlook. The male has a brown head and grey body so that it can easily be overlooked in a crowd of mallard or other ducks. The female is very like a female mallard. Both birds have a white wing-patch which is sometimes visible, but more often not! Look for the drake's black rear end and listen for its distinctive nasal call. In their modest way, drake gadwall are quite handsome and worth watching out for.

FLIGHT: The white speculum is very obvious against the brown wings and back.

SEASON: Mostly on reservoirs in winter but some stay to breed.

VOICE: Drake has a unique nasal croak "mair, mair, mair".

HABITAT: Sheltered bays and shores; rivers.
FOOD: Submerged water plants.
NEST: On ground usually near water. Breeds in the region.

Gadwall feed by picking plants from the surface and by upending in shallows. They also steal waterplants from coot which bring them up from much deeper water and this thieving lifestyle serves them well. You can't judge a bird by its respectable appearance!

WIGEON

IDENTIFICATION: Often heard before they are seen because the males have a carrying, shrill whistling call. Almost invariably in flocks, forming a dense raft on the water or feeding on grass and farmland. The male has a striking orange and yellow head with a pink breast. Females are a much richer, deeper brown than mallard and have a white tummy.

FLIGHT: Both sexes look pale in flight because of their white underparts. The drakes also have shining white patches on their forewings, unlike gadwall which have their white patches on the hindwing.

SEASON: Winter.

VOICE: Drake has a piercing, gap-toothed whistle "whee-oo".

HABITAT: Open water for roosting, grass and cereal fields for feeding.
FOOD: Grazes short grass and young cereal crops.
NEST: On the ground. Very rarely in the region.

Most of our wintering wigeon are long-distance migrants which breed in Russia, Scandinavia and Iceland. About 200,000 are present in mid-winter but less than 500 pairs stay to breed, almost all in the Highlands.

TEAL

IDENTIFICATION: Obviously smaller than other ducks. The males have a bright yellow patch under the tail which shows up at quite long distance, at least as a pale mark, even when the head pattern can't be seen. The white stripe along the side is also often conspicuous. Except in good light the handsome brown and green head simply looks dark-coloured. Females are usually a duller, deeper brown than female mallard.

FLIGHT: Springs vertically from the water and has a very fast twisting flight. A group will often sweep and turn repeatedly over the water before settling.

SEASON: Mostly winter, but birds may be present for much of the year.

VOICE: A rather high-pitched whistled "krick", more like a giant insect than a bird!

HABITAT: Very shallow water and muddy margins: well-vegetated, reed fringed pools.
FOOD: Mostly seed of aquatic plants plus insects and watersnails.
NEST: On the ground near water. Few nest in the region.

From late summer on, groups of drakes will join in communal courtship of a single female. Anything from 5 to 25 males may participate and often paired birds will leave their mates to take part. All the males go through a ritual of head shaking, tail wagging and water-flicking to win the favours of the female.

GADWALL
Length: about 50cm

Female

Male

Female

WIGEON
Length: about 48cm

Male

TEAL
Length: about 35cm

Female

Male

SHELDUCK

IDENTIFICATION: One of the largest ducks. Often looks black and white at a distance but when closer the chestnut band encircling the breast and back is obvious. Males have a red knob on the beak but otherwise both sexes look similar. Beware confusion with drake shovelers which are also green-headed and white-breasted but have chestnut sides: also they always look short-necked whereas shelduck carry their heads high. Young shelduck are pale brown and white and always seem to look worried!

FLIGHT: Dark wingtips and head contrast with the white body. Look for the chestnut breast band.

SEASON: Spring and summer. A few in winter.

VOICE: Females make a loud cackling "ak-ak-ak". The males whistle.

HABITAT: Shallow water, especially on open muddy or sandy shores and in water-treatment lagoons. Walks more easily on land than most other ducks.

FOOD: Small molluscs, insects and crustacea hoovered from wet mud or water.

NEST: In burrows, gaps in straw ricks and tree holes. A few pairs nest at reservoirs but most breed at the coast.

After breeding, groups of parents will leave their chicks in a single crèche, looked after by just one or two adults, and then fly to traditional rich feeding grounds on the Dutch coast where they briefly become flightless while moulting their old wing feathers and growing a new set.

SHOVELER

IDENTIFICATION: Notice how the shoveler's forehead slopes straight down in line with its huge beak, where all other ducks have a distinct curve between head and bill. Together with their "short-necked" look, this gives the shoveler a very distinctive shape and makes it easy to distinguish the brown females from female mallard. Like other drakes, shovelers go into "eclipse" plumage in autumn, looking rather like the females but with very rufous flanks.

FLIGHT: The drake's white breast and chestnut belly is obvious. Both sexes have pale blue patches on the upper wing surface. The size of the beak is usually easy to see.

SEASON: Autumn, winter and spring.

VOICE: Female quacks.

HABITAT: Very shallow, muddy margins of lakes and pools. Filter beds.

FOOD: Aquatic insects, snails, shrimps and seeds.

NEST: On the ground in tall cover: rare in the Anglian region.

The shoveler's beak is a complicated filtering device. Taking a beakful of water or liquid mud, the bird squirts it out sideways through interlocking filters which retain any small items of food.

GOOSANDER

IDENTIFICATION: Impressive, streamlined birds which seem to steam across the water with the confident assurance of ocean liners. The male has a pale pink or white body with a black back and a large dark green head. Females are pale grey with a chestnut head, noticeably tufted at the back. Usually seen in small parties of both sexes, the group being easy to identify by colour and shape even at long range.

FLIGHT: Both sexes look white below with a contrasting dark head and wingtips. Flying shelduck have a chestnut breastband which goosanders lack.

SEASON: Winter.

VOICE: Rarely calls except during mating display.

HABITAT: Large waterbodies in winter, upland rivers and lakes in summer.

FOOD: Fish of all sorts, mostly about 10cm long.

NEST: Uses holes in trees or among rocks. Not in the lowlands.

The goosander has a serrated edge to its long slender beak, helping it to grasp slippery prey. Often a group of birds will fish in a line or semi-circle, driving the shoal ahead of them to increase their chances of making an easy catch.

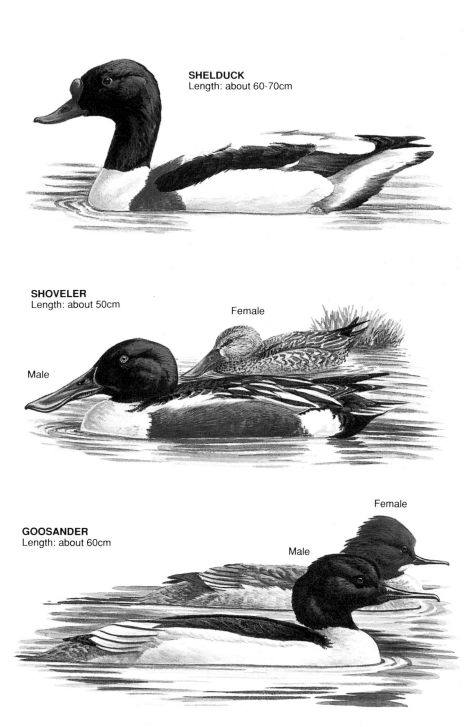

SHELDUCK
Length: about 60-70cm

SHOVELER
Length: about 50cm

Female

Male

Female

GOOSANDER
Length: about 60cm

Male

TUFTED DUCK

IDENTIFICATION: The drakes are compact black and white birds. The females are two-tone brown with a dark back and head and a slightly paler flank. Both sexes have head tufts but these are best developed on the male in winter. Some females have a conspicuous white patch at the base of the beak. Usually in flocks outside the breeding season.

FLIGHT: Both sexes show a broad white band along the rear edge of the wings. From below, drakes have a black head and tail with a brilliant white belly.

SEASON: Big flocks in winter; pairs or females with young in summer.

VOICE: Females make a harsh "kurr-kurr".

HABITAT: Open water when feeding and usually when roosting. Sometimes comes just on to the shore to rest.

FOOD: Mostly aquatic molluscs and insects obtained by diving to 1-2m.

NEST: Close to water in dense cover. Breeds in the region.

Another bird which has benefited from gravel pits and reservoirs, numbers of breeding tufted ducks in Britain have trebled since 1960 to about 7000 pairs. In winter numbers are greatly increased as about 50,000 more birds arrive from Russia, Scandinavia and Iceland.

POCHARD

IDENTIFICATION: Males are black at both ends, grey in the middle and have russet-coloured heads. Females are a very drab, sepia version of the same pattern. At first glance these birds may seem a bit like wigeon but the drake wigeon's breast is pink not black, while pochard have the compact shape typical of many diving ducks. Pochard spend much the daytime asleep, bobbing gently as if at anchor. Often seen in mixed flocks with tufted ducks.

FLIGHT: Wings greyish from above. From below like tufted ducks but the drake's fine brown head is usually obvious.

SEASON: Mostly autumn to spring: very few breed in the region.

VOICE: Usually silent.

HABITAT: Open water, usually favouring areas only about 1m deep.

FOOD: Waterplants and seeds, plus invertebrates, obtained by diving. Much feeding is done at night perhaps to avoid the thieving attentions of swans, gadwall and other plant eaters.

NEST: Placed in thick cover close to water.

The origins of some birds' names are obviously descriptive of appearance – like the tufted duck, or voice – like the coot. Others are totally mysterious. Nobody knows the origin of the pochard's name – you can pronounce it 'potchard', 'pockard' or 'poachard'. In some localities it's called a poker. One Norfolk name is smee duck!

GOLDENEYE

IDENTIFICATION: The white body of the male shows up from afar and the distinctive cheek patch is usually obvious. Females and young birds can look quite nondescript especially as the brown head colour is not always easy to see. Look carefully at the head shape which tends to be triangular rather than rounded. Also look for a short white stripe on the flank. Feeding style is also a good clue – goldeneye tend to be very active, travelling many yards with every dive and surfacing only briefly. This makes them hard to watch, incidentally!

FLIGHT: Wings make a distinctive high-pitched whistling noise. Drakes look very black and white in flight.

SEASON: Winter only.

VOICE: Mostly silent.

HABITAT: Usually on larger waters and often well offshore.

FOOD: Molluscs, insects and often invertebrates obtained by diving to depths up to 4m.

NEST: Hole in tree, mostly in Scandinavia or Russia.

By putting up nestboxes in conifer forests in Scotland, the RSPB and Forestry Commission have persuaded some goldeneye to stay to breed. There are now about 50 pairs nesting where none bred only 25 years ago.

TUFTED DUCK
Length: about 45cm

Female

Male

POCHARD
Length: about 46cm
Male

GOLDENEYE
Length: about 46cm
Male

RUDDY DUCK

IDENTIFICATION: Often the long tail is an immediate give-away, being carried erect. But as it may be lowered to the water level and become quite inconspicuous, look for the white cheek and blonde crown of the drake. In spring and summer the male has a shiny chestnut coloured body and bright blue beak. In winter the body is brown and the beak is grey. Females stay brown all year, the light cheek obscured by a dark stripe.
FLIGHT: All dark when seen from above, whereas other ducks have patterned or striped wings. Pale from below, with a darker breast-band; look for the pale cheek.
SEASON: All year, flocking in winter.
VOICE: Nearly silent except for beak rattling during courtship.

HABITAT: Open waters in winter, favouring sites with a good fringe of marginal cover for breeding.
FOOD: Invertebrates and aquatic plant seeds obtained by diving.
NEST: In dense cover, usually of evergreen plants at the water's edge.

Ruddy ducks were introduced as ornamental birds from North America and escaped to start breeding in the wild about 1960. The population has thrived and they are now about 3,000 strong.

COOT

IDENTIFICATION: All-black body with a conspicuous white forehead. The compact round shape contrasts with the much slimmer lines of moorhens. Young chicks have black down and red faces - in fact they look much like tiny moorhens. Later they develop brown plumage, again like a young moorhen but with a paler breast and face.
FLIGHT: Often runs and flaps across the waterface but rarely seen properly airborne.
SEASON: All year. Big flocks form in winter.
VOICE: The most usual call is a loud, abrupt "coot".

HABITAT: Larger waterbodies than moorhen, diving to depths of about 1-2m.
FOOD: Mostly plant material obtained by upending and diving. Coots also venture ashore to feed on grassland and on young cereal crops but race back to the water if frightened.
NEST: Floating or semi-floating platform of plant stems anchored amongst reeds or other emergent plants.

In the breeding season, coots are very aggressive. There is much skirmishing along the boundaries of adjoining territories and sometimes violent conflicts break out, male against male and female fighting female with beaks and claws. Moorhens and some other birds may be attacked and driven off.

MOORHEN

IDENTIFICATION: Easy to distinguish from the other black waterbird, the coot, by the white line along its side and by its red and yellow beak. When swimming, moorhens progress jerkily with the tail cocked up and showing two white patches beneath. Young birds are brown and buff with green beaks but have the same shape and jerky movements as the adults.
FLIGHT: Frequently flap and patter across the water but rarely fly far in daylight.
SEASON: All year.
VOICE: A loud "curruk" or "purruk" alarm call, often coming from under cover of reeds. Also squawks "kaak" or has a stuttering "kikikik-kik-kik".

HABITAT: Virtually all waterbodies of every size but does not venture far from the shore and the safety of cover. Also often feeds on land, progressing slowly and cautiously with much nervous tail-flicking.
FOOD: All sorts of insects, seeds, leaves, worms. Anything small and edible will do!
NEST: Sometimes afloat in vegetation close the bank; also on the ground in cover and sometimes well up in a tree.

Moorhens are versatile waterbirds which can run, perch in trees, swim and even dive at a pinch. They seem to do everything a bit amateurishly, always looking ungainly and self-conscious, but overall their adaptability serves them well.

RUDDY DUCK
Length: 41cm

COOT
Length: 38cm

MOORHEN
Length: 34cm

MUTE SWAN

IDENTIFICATION: Adults are massive white birds with orange and black beaks but young swans are grey at first with white plumage taking over gradually in the following winter.

FLIGHT: Flying with necks outstretched, mute swans' wings make a loud, rhythmic thrumming sound. Because of their weight, swans need a long 'run-up' to take off, wingtips beating noisily on the water surface until they are airborne.

SEASON: All year. Flocks may occur in late summer.

VOICE: An angry hissing, mostly as a warning to intruders – other swans, dogs and humans alike! Also grunting, hoarse trumpeting calls. In fact, much more vocal than their name suggests.

HABITAT: Waters up to about a metre deep.

FOOD: Water plants gathered from the surface or by upending if necessary. Also, mute swans will come ashore to graze grass and young cereals.

NEST: A massive construction of vegetation often in full view on the shore.

Most male swans don't breed until they are four years old, females at three. Birds pair for life and diligently care for their cygnets. The grey, downy youngsters often find warmth and safety riding on their mother's back.

GREYLAG GOOSE

IDENTIFICATION: A bulky brown bird with a stout orange beak. The legs and feet may be pink or orange. Reminiscent of the farmyard goose whose ancestor it is.

FLIGHT: Rapid and powerful with the neck outstretched. Wings long and rather pointed. The forewings and tail look very pale grey in good light conditions, contrasting with a dark back and hindwing.

SEASON: All year, flocking in autumn and winter.

VOICE: The familiar cackling "aanng-ang-ang" is most common but greylags have at least ten other calls and hisses, each with a special meaning.

HABITAT: Lake margins, marshes and open fields, usually retreating to open water to roost at night in safety.

FOOD: Water plants plus grass and, sometimes, other farm crops.

NEST: Built on the ground close to water in the cover of shrubs, tall grass or reeds. Pairs may nest within 2m of each other on islands.

Greylags became extinct as breeding birds in England about 1830 but they are now quite common due to a reintroduction programme by wildfowlers in the 1960s.

CANADA GOOSE

IDENTIFICATION: A large brown-bodied goose with a black neck and black and white head. Male and female are identical. The goslings are mottled yellow and brown at first but soon gain adult markings.

FLIGHT: Geese have powerful, rapid flight with the neck stretched out. Usually they travel in flocks and adopt a V-formation so that the birds 'down the line' benefit from the slipstream of those ahead of them and can fly with less effort.

SEASON: All year, with big flocks in autumn and winter.

VOICE: Loud, honking calls. Big flocks can produce an indescribable babble of noise!

HABITAT: Uses open water for safety when resting by day and roosting at night. Feeds on shoreline plants, grassland and arable farmland.

FOOD: Grazes grass and young cereals and takes the leaves and seeds of water plants.

NEST: Often built in tall vegetation or under the cover of scrub. Canada geese always use islands for nesting if possible, for protection from foxes and other predators.

First introduced to England in the 17th century, Canada geese have only become really abundant since the creation of many flooded gravel pits has provided them with ideal breeding grounds.

MUTE SWAN
Length: about 1.5m

GREYLAG GOOSE
Length: about 85cm

CANADA GOOSE
Length: about 95cm

REDSHANK

IDENTIFICATION: A noisy, nervous, long-legged brown wading bird with a mottled belly, red legs and beak. Note that birds paddling in mud may appear to have brown or black legs! Body length only slightly less than lapwing or moorhen but looks much smaller due to slender, leggy build. Usually in ones or twos when seen inland.

FLIGHT: Takes wing readily when alarmed, revealing a broad white band along the trailing edges of the wings and up the back. The only wader with this pattern.

SEASON: All year but more numerous in autumn and winter; scarce in spring and summer.

VOICE: Noisy. Quickly gives alarm at approach of predators, humans, dogs. Main call a loud "tew" note, somewhere between a yelp and a whistle in tone, usually repeated 2-4 times in rapid sequence.

HABITAT: Feeds on shorelines and in water, wading belly-deep at times. Breeds in wet grassland or marshes.

FOOD: All sorts of invertebrates mostly taken by probing wet muds and sands.

NEST: On ground concealed in tall, tussocky grass.

Formerly nesting in many riverside meadows, redshanks are now an uncommon breeding bird except on coastal saltmarshes and in nature reserves. This is due to farmland drainage since about 1950.

GREENSHANK

IDENTIFICATION: Conspicuously pale bird, being white beneath and light grey above. Slightly bigger than redshank but with a rangier, less compact build. Beak larger than redshank, slightly but visibly upcurved and dark greyish colour. Legs very long and drab green. Usually solitary.

FLIGHT: Short grey-brown wings with a wedge of white extending from the mid-back down over the tail. Slight barring on tail often not obvious. When alarmed, frequently rises very high before flying off.

SEASON: Mostly on migration in autumn; less often in spring.

VOICE: Clear, ringing "tu-tu-tu". Tone like redshank but almost invariably 3 notes where redshank varies from two to four.

HABITAT: Shorelines and shallow water.

FOOD: Insects, shrimps and other small freshwater invertebrates picked from the water surface; usually walks more rapidly and purposefully than redshank; sometimes runs after small fish in shallows.

NEST: On ground amid short heather and other vegetation in Highland bogs and Arctic tundra.

One of the special birds which breed in the Flow Country of northern Scotland over which battles have raged between forestry bodies which have ploughed up or planted much of this wilderness, and conservation bodies which wish to see it permanently protected.

LAPWING

IDENTIFICATION: At a distance appears as a plump, stocky black bird with white underparts. Closer to, the back is a most beautiful iridescent green. The crest is longest in summer. Mostly seen in flocks in autumn and winter.

FLIGHT: A very distinctive pied pattern with wings that look broadest at the ends and have notably rounded tips. Flocks manoeuvring together flash spectacularly black and white as they turn. Birds displaying on breeding territory do aerobatics with audibly "whooshing" wingbeats.

SEASON: Mostly winter flocks. Very sensitive to frost and snow; large numbers arrive in Britain when cold grips the Continent. Birds disappear westward as soon as heavy frosts occur here. A few breed on suitable short grass or bare ground.

VOICE: Unlike any other birds – a rising, two-note "pee-wit", hence its country name Peewit.

HABITAT: Open ground – ploughland, short grass or young cereals and the shores of lakes and reservoirs.

FOOD: Insects and worms picked from the ground surface. Typically birds stand still to scan for food, then move forward to pick it from the ground surface.

NEST: A scrape in bare, open ground.

Once a common breeding bird on many farms. Now very few attempt to nest because modern agriculture means grass and crops have grown too tall by early spring. Ideal conditions are ploughed ground or short-cropped turf far from hedges and trees which harbour predators such as foxes and crows.

REDSHANK
Length: 28cm

GREENSHANK
Length: 32cm

LAPWING
Length: 30cm

COMMON SANDPIPER

IDENTIFICATION: A compulsive habit of bobbing its rear end up and down makes this bird quite unmistakeable. Considerably smaller than redshank and with much shorter, dark legs. Note the brown coloration on the sides of the throat and breast, contrasting with the white underparts. Beak only a little larger than head. Usually solitary but sometimes three or four together.

FLIGHT: Typically flies very low over water, within a foot or two of the surface. The whole upperparts are dark brown with a thin white stripe along the wings – barely noticeable except at close range.

VOICE: Usually calls when disturbed or in flight – a piping three note "twee-wee-wee".

SEASON: Mainly seen during autumn migration; a few in spring.

HABITAT: Seems to avoid extremely open shores. More often feeds along margins where there are overhanging banks or adjoining cover. But sometimes perches out on exposed rocks.

FOOD: Small invertebrates usually pecked from the surface of mud or stones.

NEST: On ground in vegetation cover by upland rivers or lakes. Not in region.

Differences in leg lengths and in beak lengths and shape reflect different feeding methods in waders. Generally the larger-beaked birds probe in soft ground, upturned bills are used to grab small items in shallow water and short beaks pick from near or on the surface.

RINGED PLOVER (& LITTLE RINGED PLOVER)

IDENTIFICATION: Ringed plover is a smallish, chunky wader with a strikingly unusual head pattern, orange legs and orange and black beak. Beware confusion with the little ringed plover which is almost identical but has a dark beak and dark yellowy-brown legs. Both species are usually seen in ones or twos and feed like lapwings – first standing stock still, then scampering forward to snatch something up.

FLIGHT: A white stripe along the wings makes ringed plover somewhat like common sandpiper so look for the dark collar and head pattern. Little ringed plovers lack the wing stripe and are a drab sandy-brown on back, wings and tail.

SEASON: Ringed plovers are mostly at the coast in winter, with a few by inland waters in spring to autumn. Little ringed plovers are in Britain only from March to October.

VOICE: Both species have a range of piping whistles. Ringed plover often calls "queep", little ringed plover makes a high "pee-u".

HABITAT: Both may be seen on open shorelines, beaches, shingle but not wading in the water.

FOOD: Small invertebrates picked from the ground.

NEST: Camouflaged eggs laid in open usually on fine shingle or gravel, where the incubating bird's head pattern breaks up the outline of its head and makes it hard to see.

Little ringed plover first colonised Britain in 1938 and have spread widely where there are newly-excavated gravel pits.

DUNLIN

IDENTIFICATION: The commonest small wader, almost always in flocks, busily feeding close together. Rather nondescript in winter with greyish-brown backs and white belly. Look for the curved down tip of the beak. In spring birds may sport a black patch on the belly and this sometimes shows, at least as a mottled patch, in autumn.

FLIGHT: Thin white wing stripe like common sandpiper but back and wings are darker brown and often pale patches visible at sides of tail. Most obvious is habit of flying in close formation flocks, wheeling and turning over the water.

SEASON: Autumn to spring.

VOICE: A slurred, breathy piping "treep".

HABITAT: Open shorelines, feeding on moist mud and sand or in shallow water.

FOOD: Insect larvae, shrimps, small worms caught by probing – dunlin scurry along, pecking and probing constantly.

NEST: On ground on moorlands.

Dunlin seen in the region in winter are from Scandinavia or Siberia, but those passing through in spring and autumn are en route between nesting grounds in northern Britain, Iceland or Greenland and wintering beaches in Southern Europe and north west Africa.

COMMON SANDPIPER
Length: 20cm

RINGED PLOVER
Length: 19cm

DUNLIN
Length: 20cm

GREAT BLACK-BACKED GULL

IDENTIFICATION: These birds always look massive. Though their body length is about the same as a mallard duck, they can be nearly twice the weight and tower over most other shoreline birds. Adults have a slate black back and wings with white tips. Juveniles are mottled brown. Note especially the powerful killer's beak. You may also see dark-backed gulls which are the same size as herring gulls; these are lesser black-backed gulls. Tricky!

FLIGHT: Deceptive – looks slow because the wing beats are slow and deep but progress is rapid.

SEASON: Adults in winter; young birds sometimes in summer

VOICE: Commonest call is a deep, barking "awk-awk-awk".

HABITAT: Shorelines and open water, often well offshore.

FOOD: A powerful predator which can kill an unwary rat with one blow and swallow it whole! Also hunts coot, teal, moorhens and takes carrion such as dead fish. Visits rubbish tips.,

NEST: Mostly on offshore islands, in large colonies. Does not breed in the region.

A hunting great black-back can single out one coot in a flock and hover over it so that it dives. Then it will swoop every time the bird resurfaces until the luckless victim is exhausted and the gull quickly kills it with blows of its hatchet beak.

HERRING GULL

IDENTIFICATION: A large pale bird with a white body, light grey back and wings. The wingtips are conspicuously black with a white patch. When at rest, the folded wingtips overlap the tail and look black with white spots. In winter, many herring gulls have brown streaking on the head. To avoid confusion with common gulls, look for the sloping forehead which gives herring gulls a mean appearance. Also note the big yellow beak with its red spot and the flesh pink legs. Young herring gulls are mottled brown.

FLIGHT: Faster wing beats than great black-back. Very agile in flight. Often travel in flocks in line abreast or V-formation.

SEASON: Adults mostly in winter. Juveniles all year.

VOICE: Very varied. Typically a yelping "kyow-kyow-kyow" and a shrill "kyee-kyee-owk-yowk-yowk".

HABITAT: Shorelines, open water. Roosts offshore at night, often in massive flocks with other gulls.

FOOD: Mostly carrion and garbage in winter.

NEST: On offshore islands and cliff ledges. Also on rooftops in coastal towns.

The red spot on the beaks of herring and black-backed gulls, which imagination might suggest to be the gore of helpless victims, is actually to do with the adult's care for their fluffy young chicks. The newly-hatched baby automatically pecks at this eye-catching spot and this prompts ma or pa to regurgitate a predigested portion of baby food.

COMMON GULL

IDENTIFICATION: Though smaller, easy to confuse with herring gulls, having a pale grey back and wings, the tips of which are black with white spots. At close range look at the head shape – herring gulls have a sloping, mean-looking forehead whereas common gulls heads are round and their beaks are much smaller, making them look more cuddly (they're not, though!). Legs and beak are green. Young common gulls have grey backs, a whitish head, white tail with a black terminal bar and mottled brown wings – quite different from other young gulls.

FLIGHT: A small version of a herring gull with more rapid wing beats.

SEASON: Adults only in winter. Some young birds stay through the summer.

VOICE: Higher pitched than herring gulls, with a distinctive mewing sound.

HABITAT: Often on farmland by day, as well as foraging on shorelines. Roosts in flocks offshore at night.

FOOD: Many insects and worms, carrion, garbage in winter.

NEST: On the ground, often on moorland far from the sea. Not in the region.

Gulls are notoriously difficult to identify – one bird book deals solely with the identification of British gulls! The problems partly arise because young birds of different species often look more like each other than their own parents. Then the plumage continually changes until maturity which takes three or four years with the bigger gulls. Most birdwatchers cheat and ignore them!

GREAT BLACK-BACKED GULL
Length: about 65cm

Immature

Adult

HERRING GULL
Length: about 54cm

COMMON GULL
Length: 42cm

COMMON TERN

IDENTIFICATION: At first glance like a small, slender gull. Usually looks all white with a black cap and long tail. At close range, back and wings are very pale grey with darker wingtips, tail is forked and bill is red with a hard-to-see black tip. In late summer adults and young birds have a white forehead. When perched is very short legged and looks extremely long and slim.

FLIGHT: Often flies slowly about 2-5m above the water with head looking down. Sometimes hovers, plunges vertically to snatch small fish. Also catches insects in flight.

SEASON: Summer months only.

VOICE: Hard, insistent "kik". Grating and higher pitched "kee-yah".

HABITAT: Inland and coastal waters.

FOOD: Small fish and insects.

NEST: On bare shingle beaches, gravel pit islands, undisturbed filter beds.

The calls and songs of birds are most helpful in identification. Unfortunately they are impossible to write down properly. The only real way to learn is by watching the bird when it is actually calling. Don't try to learn more than one at a time. Unless you have an exceptional ear you will become hopelessly confused. But once you know them you can identify gulls and terns and most other birds with your eyes shut!

BLACK-HEADED GULL

IDENTIFICATION: The commonest gull in the region. Smaller than herring and common gulls. In summer, adults have chocolate-brown heads but in winter the head is white with a blackish "ear" marks. Beak and legs are red. Young birds are rather like young common gulls but have a more slender, less-rounded head shape. With a little practice these different head and beak shapes are surprisingly easy to recognise.

FLIGHT: Fast wing beats, buoyant. Look for the very obvious white streak along the leading edge of the outer half of each wing. This is the only gull with this distinctive feature, which is also clear on brownish-winged young birds, making them quite different from young common gulls.

SEASON: Most numerous in winter but some may be present all year.

VOICE: Squeals and yaps; an irritable "kwarr" and a short "kuk" note.

HABITAT: Shorelines, farmland. Big flocks roost offshore at night.

FOOD: Worms and insects, carrion, garbage, scraps.

NEST: On grassy islands in marshes. Many breed inland at sites including gravel pits.

Now you know black-headed gulls don't have black heads, herring gulls don't eat herrings & common gulls aren't that common! In fact all gulls have become more common in the last 50 years, partly because massive modern rubbish dumps provide a rich feeding ground while new reservoirs and flooded gravel pits are secure places to roost at night.

COMMON TERN
Length: 32cm

BLACK-HEADED GULL
Length: 35cm

Summer

Winter

WOODPIGEON

IDENTIFICATION: Woodpigeons in woodland almost always see you first and fly off with a startling clatter of wings. Feeding in the open they crouch, pecking busily, a cluster of plump grey shapes with white neck patches. Closer views reveal a rather beautiful bird clad in delicate pastel shades.
FLIGHT: Fast. The birds look deep-chested and show a conspicuous white bar across each upper wing.
SEASON: All year. Often in big flocks in autumn and winter.
VOICE: Five breathy cooing notes, the second one emphasised - "coo COO coo, coo-coo".

HABITAT: Breeds and roosts in woods. Feeds in open fields.
FOOD: Plants including many farm crops.
NEST: A makeshift-looking platform of twigs - you can often see the eggs through it from underneath.

Huge numbers of pigeons are shot each year but many of them would die anyway in hard weather. The survivors can breed almost year-round and rear several broods of chicks, replacing their losses.

TURTLE DOVE

IDENTIFICATION: Much smaller than woodpigeon but with the typical pigeon shape - rounded head, plump body, short legs and longish tail. Upperparts delightfully mottled brown 'tortoiseshell' colouring. Hard to see when perched in trees or scrub but flocks often perch on telegraph wires in late summer.
FLIGHT: Fast with wing tips noticeably bent back and wing beats seeming to flicker.
SEASON: Late April or early May to September.
VOICE: A sultry purring "cooorr-cooorrr-cooorr", one of the loveliest sounds of summer and a perfect lullaby for that after-picnic snooze in the sun!

HABITAT: Patches of dense scrub for nesting and cooing. Open, often rather sparsely-vegetated ground for feeding.
FOOD: Weed seeds picked from the ground. Plant leaves and bulbs.
NEST: Typical flimsy twig platform in scrub or tall hedge.

Lovers of tall, neglected hedges and wasteland where scrub springs up untended, turtle doves have declined as hedges have been cleared from farmland or cut back short.

COLLARED DOVE

IDENTIFICATION: Same size and shape as turtle dove but with a pinky-fawn back and black half collar. Much more often seen perched in the open than turtle doves and more commonly around buildings and in gardens.
FLIGHT: Similar to turtle dove with flicking beats of bent-back wings.
SEASON: All year.
VOICE: Three notes "coo-COO-cuk", often repeated ad nauseum. Also a high-pitched, nasal "skwurr" and raucous "sgwee-sgwee".
HABITAT: Suburban and village gardens, parks, picnic sites, grain stores.
FOOD: A skilful opportunist, frequenting bird

tables, livestock feeding areas and other sites where grain and other seeds are abundantly available.
NEST: Simple platform of twigs in tree or shrub.

About sixty years ago, collared doves did not occur in most of Europe. Then they began to spread west, perhaps from Yugoslavia, reaching England in the early 1950's. Though now common around villages and the fringes of towns, they are clearly very dependent on humans for much of their food supplies. The reason for the spread is not known for sure. Nor is it understood why sparrows sometimes chase them!

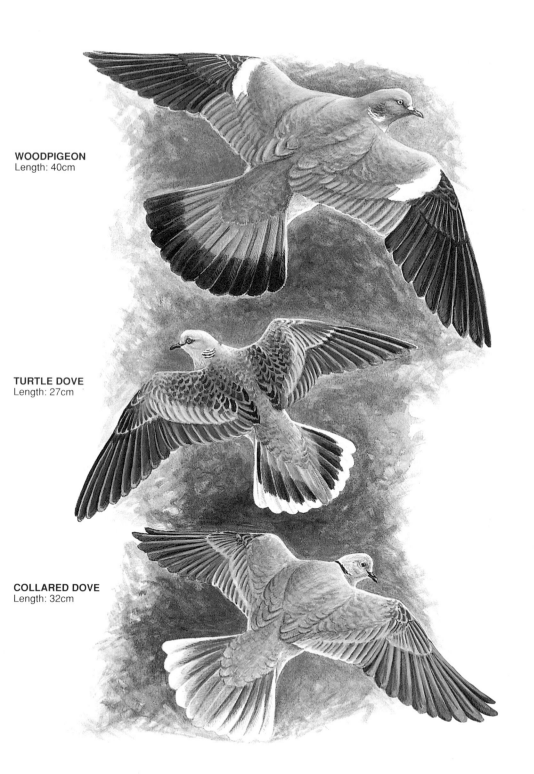

WOODPIGEON
Length: 40cm

TURTLE DOVE
Length: 27cm

COLLARED DOVE
Length: 32cm

KESTREL

IDENTIFICATION: No other large bird hovers over grassy fields and roadside verges. The male's handsome chestnut and blue coloration is also distinctive. The female's upperside is light brown with dark speckles, and pale with speckling beneath.
FLIGHT: Fast and direct with pointed wings, very long tail and large rounded head all obvious. Hovers brilliantly even in strong winds.
SEASON: All year.
VOICE: High-pitched somewhat irritable-sounding "kee-kee-kee-kee".

HABITAT: Uncut or lightly-grazed grassland, heath and moorland. Often hunts motorway verges.
FOOD: Mostly voles but all sorts of other small creatures that live in short vegetation, such as beetles and lizards. Also small birds.
NEST: In hole or fork of tree, on ledge of cliff or building, sometimes in an old crow's nest.

By hovering the kestrel can see unwary prey moving on the ground below even when it is trying to hide under cover of the grass. Kestrels will also hunt from perches such as telegraph wires when the bird's large round head and concentrated downward gaze promptly identify it.

CUCKOO

IDENTIFICATION: General colouration and shape reminiscent of a bird of prey but always perches nearly horizontally whereas kestrel (and sparrowhawk) tend to stand bolt upright. Often waves long tail from side to side.
FLIGHT: Pointed wings and long tail rather like kestrel but usually flying well below tree-top height whereas kestrel often higher. Differences in flight style, head shape and tail length obvious with experience. If in doubt, hope it calls!
SEASON: Mid April to September.
VOICE: "Cu-coo" until late June or July. Females make a noisy bubbling call and both sexes squall hoarsely when excited.

HABITAT: Very varied - trees, woodland, scrub, reedbeds, moorland and heather.
FOOD: Hairy caterpillars.
NEST: The only British bird to lay its eggs in the nest of other species - mostly small songbirds such as robin, hedge sparrow and reed warbler.

As soon as it hatches, the young cuckoo ejects other chicks or eggs from the nest to ensure that it gets all the food brought by both its foster parents. Often the chick outgrows the nest and sits atop it, noisily demanding to be fed from dawn to dusk.

SKYLARK

IDENTIFICATION: Cascading aerial song can't be missed but often the bird is so high that it's almost impossible to see. Look for it as it drops to earth, when it will probably vanish again, crouching and creeping away amongst grass tussocks or crops. When seen, looks plump and often raises a bluntly triangular crest.
FLIGHT: Mounts almost vertically to sing, then hovers before sinking down and finally dropping swiftly to earth.
SEASON: All year. May be in flocks in autumn and winter.
VOICE: Far-carrying, sustained warbling song. Call note is a liquid rippling "chirrup".

HABITAT: Grasslands and farm crops.
FOOD: Seeds, insects and worms.
NEST: Cup of grasses concealed in a tussock.

Male birds have to advertise their possession of territory both to attract a mate and deter other males from moving in. By flying high to sing, the male skylark advertises his presence as widely as possible in a habitat without perches.

KESTREL
Length: 35cm
Male

CUCKOO
Length: 33cm

SKYLARK
Length: 18cm

Song flight

SWALLOW

IDENTIFICATION: Perches upright, usually on telegraph wires, when the long tail streamers are clearly visible. Note also the brick red face and blue chest band. Though house martins have similar blue-black wings and back they have a white chin and throat, a white rump and a short, notched tail.
FLIGHT: Often within a metre of the ground. Look for the all-dark back and tail streamers.
SEASON: Mostly April to September.
VOICE: Excited, staccato "tswit, tswit". Twittering song both when perched and in flight.

HABITAT: Feeds over farmland and open water. Autumn flocks gather on wires and sometimes big flocks roost in reedbeds.
FOOD: Insects caught in flight.
NEST: A mud cup placed on a beam or projection in an open outbuilding or barn.

Before it was proved that birds migrate, it was believed that swallows spent the winter hibernating in the mud on the bottom of farm ponds.

HOUSE MARTIN

IDENTIFICATION: The most obvious distinguishing marks are the white rump, clean white underparts and short, notched tail.
FLIGHT: Usually higher than swallows - sometimes almost at the limits of sight (but swifts go much higher). Groups of birds seem to swirl around the sky as individuals twist and turn in the flock.
SEASON: Mainly April to September.
VOICE: A spluttering "chichirrp" and "chirrp" often noisily repeated by birds in a flock. If you hear the pitch rising to a nervous squeak, and the flock bunches in the sky, it means a hunting bird of prey is about.

HABITAT: Often over towns and villages, where nests are sited. Also feeds over water, woods and farmland. Gathers in flocks on wires, roofs, trees in autumn.
FOOD: Small insects caught in flight.
NEST: A mud structure with a small entrance hole at the top, stuck under the eaves of a building. Usually several nests close together and sometimes large colonies on a single house.

House Martins must have been much rarer before humans began to build houses. They do nest in caves but the number of natural sites is tiny compared with the "unnatural" opportunities created by man.

SAND MARTIN

IDENTIFICATION: An insignificant little brown bird all too easily overlooked. Note the brown chest band and the uniformly brown upperparts without a white rump. Tail slightly notched.
FLIGHT: Almost always over water with jerky rather weak-looking wingbeats, weaving and jinking in pursuit of insects.
SEASON: An early arriver, usually present by late March and staying to September or October.
VOICE: Sharp, dry "chrrp".

HABITAT: Rivers and flooded gravel pits when breeding. Anywhere over water on migration.
FOOD: Mostly aquatic insects caught in flight.
NEST: A tunnel about 1 m long excavated by both adults in firm but soft ground or sand in the eroded banks of rivers or sides of gravel and sand pits.

Numbers of this bird crashed in the early 1970's due to the drought in the southern fringes of the Sahara where sand martins spend the winter. Recent years have seen some recovery.

SWALLOW
Length: 20cm

HOUSE MARTIN
Length: 13cm

SAND MARTIN
Length: 12 cm

SWIFT

IDENTIFICATION: A black, stiff-winged, crescent shaped flying machine that feeds, sleeps and mates on the wing and looks like it. At a casual glance could be confused with Swallows and martins but relative proportions of large wings and short-tailed body very different from them.
FLIGHT: Wings seem to flicker as rapid beats propel the bird across the sky. Can go very low or high beyond the limits of sight. Usually several in view - sometimes dozens.
SEASON: The last summer migrant to arrive and the first to leave - mid May to August mostly.
VOICE: Excited, shrill screaming.

HABITAT: Nests in cavities in roofs of buildings and feeds aerially, often over water.
FOOD: Airborne insects.
NEST: Shallow cup of grass, leaves and feathers cemented together with saliva.

If poor weather limits local availability of flying insects, adult swifts may commute as far as 50 kms to collect food, bringing back up to 1000 individual insects packed together in a ball in the back of the throat to feed their young.

KINGFISHER

IDENTIFICATION: Usually seen as a flash of electric blue streaking past low over the water. When perched the orange underparts are very conspicuous but the bird is fairly small and keeps so still it is easily overlooked.
FLIGHT: Swift and direct, usually within 1 m of water surface.
SEASON: All year. Most likely to be seen at reservoirs in winter.
VOICE: Shrill, piping "chee" which often gives you warning that a bird is flying past in time to get at least a quick glimpse.

HABITAT: All water bodies with small fish. Usually fishes by diving from overhanging branch but will sometimes hover over open water.
FOOD: Small fish up to 8 cm long.
NEST: A pile of fishbones at the end of a tunnel excavated in the bank of a river or gravel pit.

Learning to catch enough fish is not easy. Many young kingfishers drown or starve when first left to fend for themselves. In freezing conditions adults too die in large numbers.

GREEN WOODPECKER

IDENTIFICATION: More often heard than seen. In flight the brilliant yellow rump is most obvious but often the red head is not seen as the bird flies away. Hard to watch when in a tree as it hides behind the trunk and peers cautiously round it.
FLIGHT: Bounding, with brief bursts of flaps interspersed by long swooping glides.
SEASON: All year.
VOICE: Laughing "yaffle" which carries long distances. Once called the rainbird because it was believed to call when rain is about to fall.

HABITAT: Woodland or parkland with big trees, usually near grassland heaths or commons.
FOOD: Mostly ants and their larvae and pupae.
NEST: A cavity excavated in the trunk or large branch of a tree.

The green woodpecker's tongue is 10 cm long and it has sticky saliva so that it can "harpoon" ant pupae deep inside the ants' nest.

SWIFT
Length: 17cm

KINGFISHER
Length: 17cm

GREEN WOODPECKER
Length: 32cm

BARN OWL

IDENTIFICATION: Seen perched at the entrance to a tree cavity the barn owl is unmistakable but in flight at dawn or dusk the bird looks so white you might mistake it for a gull, though the style of flying is quite different. In the glare of car headlights, tawny owls can look very pale and confusion between the two species is possible.

FLIGHT: When hunting, low, slow and very buoyant, quartering the ground. Swift and direct when returning to nest with prey. Wings large and rounded, not pointed like gulls. Large head also very obvious.

SEASON: All year. Most likely to be seen before dusk or after dawn in summer when feeding owlets.

VOICE: Snoring sounds and horrid shrieks.

HABITAT: Rough grassland including field edges, on woodland rides and roadside verges.

FOOD: Small mammals, mainly voles and shrews.

NEST: In tree cavity or on ledge in undisturbed barn or other building. Uses nestboxes.

Barn owls catch much prey by hearing rather than sight. The round facial disc helps to pick up faint squeals and rustles from deep within the cover of tall grass.

MAGPIE

IDENTIFICATION: Combination of pied plumage, long tail and large size makes magpies instantly identifiable. Male and female look identical.

FLIGHT: Alternating rapid beats and long glides, usually over short distances.

SEASON: All year

VOICE: Rattling, rapid "chaka-chaka-chaka-chaka". Sometimes several birds racketing together. Rarely solitary - usually in twos in spring but varied size flocks in other seasons. Hence all the rhymes - "One for sorrow, two for mirth, etc".

HABITAT: Grassland with livestock, woodland, big hedges, scrub, shorelines.

FOOD: Almost anything - insects and worms, eggs, nestlings, small mammals and reptiles, carrion (especially road casualties), berries, seeds and fruit.

NEST: A large structure carefully domed with twigs as a protection against other nest-robbers! Often low and obvious in scrub or hedgerow tree.

The magpie's skill in finding the nests of pheasant and partridge make it loathed by gamekeepers who legally kill large numbers. Nonetheless, being artful and wary birds, many manage to survive and breed successfully each year.

PHEASANT

IDENTIFICATION: Cock bird usually very easy to identify, though plumages vary - some lack the white neck ring, others are almost black. Hens are much smaller and mottled brown but the long tail is a certain clue.

FLIGHT: Often run for cover when disturbed in the open. Forced to fly, the bird rockets away with whirring wings.

SEASON: All year. Most obvious in late autumn before shooting starts.

VOICE: Cocks crow "koork-kok" and make a staccato "kutuk...kutuk". Audible at long range.

HABITAT: Broadleaved woodland, farm fields and marshes.

FOOD: Seeds or invertebrates.

NEST: On ground concealed in the cover of woodland plants.

Pheasants come from Asia and were introduced here about 900 years ago, or perhaps much earlier by the Romans. Today, vast numbers are reared artificially and released for shooting over the following winter.

BARN OWL
Length: 34cm

MAGPIE
Length: 45cm

PHEASANT
Length: Male about 80cm
Female: about 60cm

CARRION CROW

IDENTIFICATION: Usually solitary or in pairs. All black without white face or shaggy belly feathers of rook.
FLIGHT: Hard to distinguish from solitary rook but head looks less elongated and wingbeats often a bit slower, giving an impression of "trudging" along.
SEASON: All year.
VOICE: A bit harsher and deeper-pitched than rook's caw. Where a single rook may call once or a flock will produce a jumble of calls, a crow is likely to give 3 or 4 deliberate "kraa" calls in succession.

HABITAT: Everywhere, but usually very wary of humans.
FOOD: Everything but mainly insects, eggs, carrion.
NEST: A conspicuous stick structure, usually in a tree.

Long persecuted by man, carrion crows are hard to approach within gunshot range. Their two main enemies are gamekeepers, protecting pheasant and partridge nests, and hill sheep farmers who believe that crows kill many new-born lambs.

JACKDAW

IDENTIFICATION: Smaller than rook or crow, with a more compact build and a shorter, less-powerful beak. The blue-grey nape is very obvious in good light but can be overlooked when the bird is at a distance. Often feeds and flies with rooks.
FLIGHT: Quicker wingbeats than rook or crow, without obvious wingtip "fingers".
SEASON: All year.
VOICE: A ringing, cheery "Jack" and a shrill "kya". Often several birds will call noisily together.

HABITAT: Farmland and woodland. Also seacliffs and crags.
FOOD: Like rook and crow, virtually omnivorous. Mostly, insects and seeds on ground but also fruit and berries and not averse to birdnesting in spring.
NEST: Pile of sticks in any sort of hole or crevice in tree or rocks or down a chimney.

Gregarious birds which sometimes nest in big colonies and usually feed in flocks, Jackdaws nonetheless stay closest to their own mates and, whether in flight or foraging on the ground, you can usually see that the birds stay "two by two".

ROOK

IDENTIFICATION: "If you see a lot of crows they're rooks. If you see one rook, it's a crow". Rooks flock and nest colonially. Adult rooks have white faces - though young ones don't. All rooks wear shaggy "trousers".
FLIGHT: Continuous wingbeats with a deep downstroke often showing separated "fingers" (primary feathers) at the wingtip.
SEASON: All year round.
VOICE: A deep, pleasant cawing. In spring, courting birds make odd squawks and undignified yelps.

HABITAT: Farmland especially ploughed fields, newly-cut hayfields and short grass such as pasture.
FOOD: A very wide range but mostly insects from soil or grass, grain, some carrion.
NEST: A strong nest of sticks and twigs - some carried from afar, some filched from unwary neighbours. Rookeries usually in small copses rather than large woods: often in villages.

Rooks have become amazingly adept at feeding on roadsides right besides fast-moving traffic. Here in summer they pick up the 'rain' of dead insects hit by cars and in winter frosts feed on the salt-thawed verges.

CARRION CROW
Length: 47cm

JACKDAW
Length: 33cm

ROOK
Length: 46cm

GREAT TIT

IDENTIFICATION: The white cheek ringed with navy blue tends to show up whatever the bird is doing. Look also for the navy stripe down the chest and belly: this is wider in males than females.
FLIGHT: Strong and undulating.
SEASON: All year.
VOICE: A wide repertoire of metallic notes including "chink" very like chaffinch's call. Song is ringing, repeated "teacher...teacher...teacher".

HABITAT: Woodlands, hedges, scrub, gardens.
FOOD: Invertebrates, berries, seeds.
NEST: Concealed in a hole in a tree.

Larger than blue tits, great tits feed much more on the ground where they busily turn over dead leaves, small twigs and other woodland litter to search for concealed insects, worms or seeds. The strong, stout beak can break open beech mast and even hack through the shell of a hazel nut while the bird holds it steady under one foot. In summer their diet changes to insects found in foliage and the chicks are reared on caterpillars.

BLUE TIT

IDENTIFICATION: The bright blue crown and wings are immediately recognisable. In spring these little birds are positively jewel-like. Blue tits are very active, acrobatic birds - busy in the treetops and almost always vocal.
FLIGHT: Flits between trees. Undulating and quite strong when travelling over open ground.
SEASON: All year.
VOICE: Always has something to say. Usually "tsee-tsee-tsit" or persistent churring. Song "tsee-tsee-tsee" followed by a trill.

HABITAT: Woodland, scrub, hedges.
FOOD: Mostly insects and spiders but also seeds and, of course, peanuts. Mostly feeds off the ground.
NEST: Concealed in a hole in a tree or, sometimes, a wall or pipe.

Blue tits become nomadic once the nesting season ends and wander widely along hedges and from wood to wood. A garden bird feeder may be visited by dozens or hundreds of different blue tits in the course of a winter.

LONG-TAILED TIT

IDENTIFICATION: The tiny, fluffed out body and ridiculously long tail create a very endearing picture as the birds flit busily along a hedge. The pale pink colouration is quite noticeable.
FLIGHT: Almost constantly on the move, flying from branch to branch and from one bush to the next. Often in flocks which give the impression of being blown along as bird after bird flits rapidly past you down a hedgeline or through a patch of scrub.
SEASON: All year. In family groups and flocks outside the breeding season, sometimes with other tits.
VOICE: Often first noticed because of contact calls between birds, which are a distinctive "putt...putt" sound.

HABITAT: Scrub, bramble patches, hedges, woodland.
FOOD: Mostly small insects, such as aphids and spiders picked from twigs and foliage.
NEST: An enclosed oval made of moss woven together with hair and cobwebs, camouflaged with lichens and lined with huge numbers of small feathers - typically about 1500 but sometimes over 2000.

Because they are so small, long-tailed tits could easily freeze to death on cold winter's nights. To help retain their body warmth groups of them huddle together like a feathery ball with only their tails sticking out. Even so, many do die in prolonged freezing conditions.

GREAT TIT
Length: 14cm

BLUE TIT
Length: 11cm

LONG-TAILED TIT
Length: 14cm

MISTLE THRUSH

IDENTIFICATION: Larger than song thrush or redwing, looking paler and more grey. Spotting extends right under belly. Has a particularly upright stance when on the ground and moves with vigorous bounding hops.

FLIGHT: Very undulating, alternating flaps and glides. Look for the white underwing.

SEASON: All year. May be in small flocks in autumn and winter but rarely with other thrushes.

VOICE: Rattling, aggressive alarm. Song a strongly delivered sequence of melodious phrases, more complex than song thrush but the same tone. Usually the first song of spring, delivered from the topmost branch of a tree from January on.

HABITAT: Woodland and gardens. Likes big expanses of short turf such as golf courses and parks.

FOOD: Invertebrates found on the ground; berries and fruit.

NEST: Open cups usually in fork of tree close to trunk. A very early breeder - young may have left the nest before April arrives!

Birds of great character, mistle thrushes sing cheerfully in defiance of the cold, blustering winds of winter - hence their name "Storm cock" - and defend their nests boldly against intruding magpies, cats and even humans

FIELDFARE

IDENTIFICATION: A large, strikingly plumaged thrush. Look for the grey head and dark tail, rich brown wings and, often, orange flush on breast. Flying off, birds show a slate grey back. Often in mixed flocks with redwings.

FLIGHT: Usually in flocks, each few flaps followed by a smooth glide.

SEASON: Arrives September and stays until April.

VOICE: Noisy chattering "chak-chak-chak" often draws attention to feeding or flying birds.

HABITAT: Grassland, hedges or scrub with berries, orchards with unpicked apples.

FOOD: Worms and other invertebrates, berries, fruit.

NEST: Very small numbers breed in the Pennines and Scotland but most of our wintering birds return to Scandinavia to breed. The nest is an open cup placed in a tree.

Many birds feed in flocks in winter. One benefit is that many eyes make for safety. It is hard for an individual to search for food and keep watch for predators at the same time but in a group one or other bird is usually alert and its alarm call will put the rest to instant flight.

REDWING

IDENTIFICATION: Very similar to song thrush but only present in autumn and winter and almost always in noisy flocks, often with fieldfares. Look for two conspicuous features - the pale stripes on the face and the red underwing.

FLIGHT: The underwing colour is usually easy to see and a much stronger rufous tone than the buff underside of the song thrush's wing.

SEASON: September to April.

VOICE: Chattering "chuttuck" calls from flocks. In flight a drawn out, sibilant "tseeip" often to be heard at night as birds fly overhead on migration.

HABITAT: Mostly grassland plus hedges and scrub with berries, and orchards. Roosts in scrub and woods.

FOOD: Invertebrates picked from the ground. Berries and fruit.

NEST: Only a handful breed here, all in northern Scotland.

Redwings are nomadic in winter. Birds from Scandinavia which winter here in one year may be in the countries round the eastern Mediterranean next year. Basically, they quickly move away from bad weather and stop when they find good feeding.

MISTLE THRUSH
Length: 27cm

FIELDFARE
Length: 26cm

REDWING
Length: 21cm

BLACKBIRD

IDENTIFICATION: The cock is glossy black with a handsome yellow beak and eye ring. Females are a warm brown with dark speckles on throat and breast.
FLIGHT: Usually flies low but may be seen crossing open fields at treetop height or more. Looks long-tailed compared with starling.
SEASON: All year.
VOICE: Male has a rich fluting song, varied, melodious and prolonged. Both sexes have hysterical "pinking" alarm and leisurely "chink-chink" roosting call at dusk.

HABITAT: Woodland, scrub and gardens. Also feeds in fields but usually close to cover.
FOOD: Fruit, berries and invertebrates scuffled out of soft ground or leaf litter. Rummages noisily under bushes.
NEST: Open cup in bush, hedge or tree usually within 3 m of ground.

Huge numbers of blackbirds fall prey to cats and many more die from other causes including winter starvation. Even so, blackbirds maintain their numbers, rearing 2 or 3 broods of perhaps 4 or 5 young every year.

STARLING

IDENTIFICATION: In autumn and winter has a dark beak and body with very obvious white spots and dark beak. In spring looks more glossy with much smaller spangles and a yellow beak. Young birds are mousey brown. Note the distinctive short tail, upright stance and waddling walk - like a bird with its hands clasped behind its back.
FLIGHT: Alternate bursts of flaps, then glides, but direct, not dipping. Wings are broad-based and pointed at tip so appear triangular.
SEASON: All year. From late summer to spring often in flocks sometimes many thousands strong.
VOICE: Cheerful whistling, trilling and mimicry of other birds, police cars and telephones.

HABITAT: Grassland, ploughed or newly-sown farmland, sewage farms, gardens. Often at birdtables. Woodlands and buildings to nest. Woods, reedbeds and town centres for roosting flocks in winter.
FOOD: Invertebrates especially leatherjackets - the larvae of craneflies - in lawns and other grassland, grain and other seeds, fruit.
NEST: In hole in tree or building.

Often ignored because they are so numerous, starlings deserve a second look. The spring plumage is gorgeously iridescent, the song jolly and the vast flocks are really dramatic when in flight.

SONG THRUSH

IDENTIFICATION: Confusion with mistle thrush and redwing is possible. Note how the song thrush has brown upperparts with spotting on breast and flanks while mistle thrushes look greyer on head and back and have bolder spotting extending right onto the belly.
FLIGHT: Alternate flaps and glides. In flight, song thrush has a fawn coloured underwing but mistle thrush's is white and redwing's is conspicuous reddish brown.
SEASON: All year.
VOICE: A pleasant, strong whistling, not so fluty as blackbird. Often each phrase is repeated 2-3 times. Listen for "Pretty Joey.....Pretty Joey".

HABITAT: Woodland, scrub, gardens, grassland.
FOOD: Mainly invertebrates including worms and snails. Breaks open snail shells by bashing them on stones.
NEST: An open cup, mud lined, in a bush or tree.

Some song thrushes which breed here winter in southwest Europe. Others arrive here from Scandinavia to overwinter. Yet others simply pass through in autumn and spring en route between, perhaps, Spain and Norway. So despite its plump, stay-at-home air, the song thrush can be a great traveller.

Female

BLACKBIRD
Length: 25cm
Male

STARLING
Length: 22cm

SONG THRUSH
Length: 23cm

SEDGE WARBLER

IDENTIFICATION: More often heard than seen, the sedge warbler is usually glimpsed briefly, perched on the edge of a dense bush or bramble patch close to the water before it ducks out of sight and scolds you noisily from deep cover.
FLIGHT: Swift and low, diving out of one bush and into the next.
SEASON: April to September.
VOICE: A fast, sustained jumble of sweet and harsh or churring notes mixed with brief mimicry of other bird's calls, such as pied wagtail and lapwing. Sometimes when singing flies up above bush and then drops down again. Stuttering scolding call.

HABITAT: Dense scrub, brambles, tall herbage close to water.
FOOD: Insects.
NEST: Deep cup low down in thick vegetation.

Sedge warblers have a remarkable migration strategy. In autumn they congregate in reed beds where they feed continuously on the plum-reed aphids. This enables them to lay down large deposits of fat which are the "fuel" for long-distance flight. Birds may even double their weight at this stage. They can then make their journey to wintering grounds south of the Sahara almost non-stop.

WILLOW WARBLER (& CHIFFCHAFF)

IDENTIFICATION: Another bird more often heard than seen, the spring song cascades from every stand of newly-greening trees. Looks very small and drab yellowish-green. Often the pale eyestripe is difficult to see as the bird slips busily through the foliage.
FLIGHT: Usually flitting quickly from tree to tree.
SEASON: April to September.
VOICE: A sweet and rapid song from the treetops in April and May. Starting quietly, in a few notes it grows louder and then drops away to a final flourish.

HABITAT: Woodland, stands of birch trees and willows with rough grass or tangled herbage beneath.
FOOD: Insects gleaned from the foliage of trees and bushes.
NEST: Domed construction hidden in a grass tussock or similar cover.

As well as the willow warbler a bird almost identical in appearance also arrives in our woods in April. Fortunately its song is totally different- a repeated "chiff-chaff...chiff-chaff" which gives the bird its name - the chiffchaff.

WREN

IDENTIFICATION: Often no more than a little brown blur slipping quickly through the tangle of a hedgebottom, or a burst of song from somewhere out of sight. A good view reveals the short, cocked tail, dumpy body and needle-sharp beak.
FLIGHT: Direct, usually very close to the ground, like a little ball with whirring wings.
SEASON: All year.
VOICE: Surprisingly loud for one so small. Song is a rapid burst of musical notes ending with a trill. Scolds humans from cover with an irritable churring.

HABITAT: Very common in woods, scrub and good thick hedges. Forages through almost any rough cover in winter, including reedbeds and ditch bottoms. Also abundant in upland heather and bracken.
FOOD: Small invertebrates winkled out of crannies with the slender beak.
NEST: A spherical structure with a small entrance hole - usually brilliantly concealed low down in a crevice or amongst ivy.

Wrens build several nests and offer the female a choice. She selects one for her eggs. Then, rather than waste the rest, some males offer them to other females and thus contrive to father two or three broods at a time.

SEDGE WARBLER
Length: 13cm

WILLOW WARBLER
Length: 11cm

WREN
Length: 10cm

REED BUNTING

IDENTIFICATION: Males are easy in summer, the black head and white 'moustache' contrasting with a warm brown back. In winter, the black becomes a patchy grey-brown. Females have brown heads with a distinct pale stripe through the eye and a streaky "moustache".
FLIGHT: Often jerky and weak-looking. Sometimes low but also rises high before swooping into cover. White outer tail feathers often obvious when flying.
SEASON: All year.
VOICE: Song a few wheezy notes, delivered slowly and then repeated after pauses. A strong contender for the most boring birdsong.
HABITAT: Almost always by water in marshes and on shores but also in nearby hedges, scrub or rough grassland.
FOOD: Seeds and insects mostly taken from the ground.
NEST: On or near ground in bush or tussock.

Most birds change their diets with the seasons. For small songbirds, insects are abundant and nutritious in spring and summer but are replaced by seeds in autumn and winter. Most competition between different species is avoided by their feeding in different places, for instance reed bunting in damp areas, yellowhammer mostly in dry ones.

HOUSE SPARROW

IDENTIFICATION: Usually seen so close to that the males at least are easy to recognise despite their rather dull appearance. Note the grey crown and, in spring, the black bib. Females have drab underparts, streaky brown backs and a broad pale stripe over the eye. Almost always puffs out feathers and looks comfortably plump.
FLIGHT: Rapid beats, direct or undulating.
SEASON: All year but only in countryside in late summer.
VOICE: The familiar "chee-ip" plus a repertoire of other chirps and twitters.

HABITAT: Towns, villages, parks and gardens. Rarely far from human dwellings.
FOOD: Seeds and insects garnered from the ground.
NEST: Untidy ball of grasses or straw usually in a cavity on a building.

How often are small brown birds in the countryside dismissed as "sparrows"? Yet they very rarely are. House sparrows are highly dependent on humans and their gardens for food, only venturing out onto farmland when grain is ripening in late summer; then they are usually much more wary and flighty than in the familiar security of their own back yards!

DUNNOCK or HEDGE SPARROW

IDENTIFICATION: A little, mousey brown bird creeping about under a bush just about sums it up. But worth a second glance for the delicacy of the brown streaking and the soft blue-grey colouration of the head and breast.
FLIGHT: Usually short flips between bushes.
SEASON: All year.
VOICE: Spring song is a pleasing short warble, often repeated over and over by a bird sitting on top of a bush or hedge. Listen for it in March before the summer migrants arrive to drown it out - and confuse you!

HABITAT: Bushes giving cover close to ground, in gardens, hedges, woods and scrub. Rarely ventures far into the open.
FOOD: Small invertebrates and seeds picked from the ground. Dunnocks shuffle about like a short-sighted bird looking for 5p.
NEST: An open cup set low in a bush with 4 - 5 exquisite turquoise blue eggs.

Everything about this bird's looks and demeanour suggest a modest, retiring life. Far from it! Many dunnocks have amazingly complicated sex lives. A male may mate with up to 3 females. Or a female may have 2 or 3 males. Sometimes several males and several females may all mate with each other. Perhaps they shuffle because they're exhausted.

REED BUNTING
Length: 15cm
Male

HOUSE SPARROW
Length: 15cm
Male

DUNNOCK
Length: 14cm

YELLOWHAMMER

IDENTIFICATION: The male's bright yellow head and front are very conspicuous. Its back is a rich brown and the bright chestnut rump is noticeable if the bird flies up ahead of you. The female is a discreetly duller version of the male. Perches upright. Often feeds on ground where it seems to crouch and is easy to overlook
FLIGHT: Sometimes undulating, sometimes direct.
SEASON: All year. Often in small flocks in winter.
VOICE: A rapid run of notes usually ending with a wheezy "chwee", invariably described as "a-little-bit-of-bread-and-no-cheese". Usually sung from an obvious perch high in a bush or hedgerow tree.

HABITAT: Farmland with good thick hedges; scrub; rough grassland.
FOOD: Seeds and insects mostly picked from the ground and among grass tussocks.
NEST: Neat cup on or close to ground. Eggs covered in fine, dark lines, hence the old-fashioned name "Scribbling Lark".

Hen birds are usually drabber than their mates because they need to be able to conceal themselves when incubating eggs. By contrast, males don bright colours to make themselves obvious to defend their territories and attract mates.

PIED WAGTAIL

IDENTIFICATION: A very distinctive small black and white bird with a long tail, constantly wagged up and down. Runs rapidly along shorelines or over short grass. Young birds are rather drab grey and buff but their shape and behaviour are just like the adults.
FLIGHT: Undulating. Often only a few feet above the ground or water. Long, slender tail always obvious.
SEASON: All year.
VOICE: Loud, confident "chissik" often given in flight hence its dreadful name "Chiswick flyover".

HABITAT: Shorelines, bare ground, short turf and car parks usually near water. Winter roosts by flocks in reedbeds and other sheltered cover.
FOOD: Insects, mostly picked from ground by scurrying bird.
NEST: Concealed in a cavity or hole in a bank, wall or tree stump. Sometimes in buildings.

In winter, night-time cold can quickly kill small birds unless they find sheltered spots where their insulating plumage is not ruffled by wind. Pied wagtails are very skilful at this and some flocks regularly use heated greenhouses or boiler rooms if they can gain access.

YELLOW WAGTAIL

IDENTIFICATION: The cock bird is brilliant yellow. The only possibility of confusion is with the male yellowhammer but note the wagtail's sleek, long-tailed shape and running gait. Yellowhammers look chubby by comparison and they hop around. Female yellow wagtails are a paler yellow with browny-green upperparts.
FLIGHT: Typical bouncing wagtail action, often low over grass or water.
SEASON: Mostly May to September. Often large numbers arrive together on the same spring day.
VOICE: Assertive "tswee-ip", not unlike pied wagtail's call.

HABITAT: Poorly-drained riverside meadows. Sometimes in arable crops or amenity grassland at reservoirs. Perches in trees more than pied wagtail.
FOOD: Insects snatched from short herbage or, by upward flip, when rashly flying close overhead.
NEST: Concealed in tussocky grass.

Wagtails run because they catch quick-moving insects in very open habitats. Yellowhammers, like most small birds, hop because they look for seeds or slow-moving insects in tall grass where walking is impossible for them.

YELLOWHAMMER
Length: 16cm
Male

PIED WAGTAIL
Length: 18cm

Female

YELLOW WAGTAIL
Length: 17cm
Male

GOLDFINCH

IDENTIFICATION: A most brilliant little bird with a delicate build, scarlet face and golden bars along its wings. Young birds have the yellow and black wings but their heads are only a dullish pale brown. Often seen feeding acrobatically on thistle or teasel heads.
FLIGHT: Bouncy and erratic - rather as if the birds were being blown along by a gust of wind.
SEASON: Spring to autumn with only a few overwintering - most go to western France and NW Spain.
VOICE: A distinctive, liquid twittering.

HABITAT: Weedy ground such as woodland fringes, building sites and waste ground.
FOOD: Weed seeds including thistles, ragwort and burdock.
NEST: High in the crotch of a small tree. Sometimes several pairs may nest close together.

Being so attractive, goldfinches have been introduced to several countries including Australia, New Zealand, Argentina and Bermuda. It was once a popular cage bird here but it is now illegal to capture wild birds without a special licence.

GREENFINCH

IDENTIFICATION: Often the most striking features are the yellow patches in the wings and tail but the general appearance of a stocky yellow, green and grey bird is very different from the unmistakable slender shape of the gold and black goldfinches. In winter, greenfinches can look very dull - almost browny-grey.
FLIGHT: Usually undulating. Watch out for the cock bird's spring display flight, circling round treetops with slow wingbeats like a huge butterfly.
SEASON: All year. Often in flocks outside the nesting season.
VOICE: Most distinctive call is a long-drawn nasal "dzwee".

HABITAT: Tall hedges, scrub, woodland edges, parks and large gardens.
FOOD: Mostly large seeds and berries.
NEST: Cup placed at about head height in bushes or small trees.

Because they have relatively large, strong beaks, greenfinches mostly take larger seeds than goldfinches or linnets and also feed on berries. Like all birds, their diet changes with the seasons and includes the seeds of burdock, dandelions, brambles and wild roses, yew and elm trees. They also eat ripening grain and empty peanut bags at great speed

LINNET

IDENTIFICATION: The cock linnet's handsome red breast and forehead are donned only for the breeding season. For the rest of the year males are like females - small streaky brown birds. But the pale bar along the edge of the closed wing, plus the black tail, are good guides to identity.
FLIGHT: Bouncing but rather more rapid and purposeful in appearance than the erratic swirl of goldfinches.
SEASON: All year. Flocking outside the nesting season.
VOICE: Rapid twitter in flight "chichichichit", not so liquid as goldfinch.

HABITAT: Open ground with small weedy plants, gorse thickets, scrub.
FOOD: Small seeds and insects.
NEST: Cup often low in bush. Gorse is especially favoured for nesting.

Once extremely common, linnets have declined and become quite scarce in some areas. This is because of the efficiency of modern farm herbicides which remove most of the weeds which they rely on for food. Now often most numerous on undeveloped building sites around towns and villages.

GOLDFINCH
Length: 12cm

GREENFINCH
Length: 15cm

LINNET
Length: 14cm
Male

BULLFINCH

IDENTIFICATION: Despite the male's magnificent rose-red breast, bullfinches can easily be overlooked as they tend to keep in bushy cover. The female's breast is a subdued pastel pink. Note the bullneck and heavy beak.

FLIGHT: Most often seen flitting into cover, when the birds reveal a conspicuous white rump patch which contrasts with the black tail and grey back.

SEASON: All year.

VOICE: A plaintive, low piping "teeu".

HABITAT: Scrub, well grown hedges, woodland, orchards.

FOOD: Berries, seeds, buds and insects.

NEST: Open cup concealed in thick bushes or brambles.

Bullfinches can be serious pests in commercial fruit orchards because they will strip trees and soft fruit bushes of their buds in early spring. However, the birds prefer to feed on wild plants such as the seeds of ash trees, the flowers of oak and sallow and the seeds of docks. When these are abundant, damage in orchards is much less.

CHAFFINCH

IDENTIFICATION: One of the commonest birds of woods or gardens. In spring, the cock is splendidly clad in pale blue, chestnut and yellow-green with distinctive double white wingbars. The hen is a delicate brownish-green but has the same white wingbars.

FLIGHT: Undulating. Again, the double wing bars are very noticeable.

SEASON: All year.

VOICE: Insistent, metallic "spink...spink". Spring song oft-repeated, rapid "chip-chip-chip-chwee-chwee-tissi-chooe-oo".

HABITAT: Woods, hedges with trees or tall shrubs, scrub, gardens.

FOOD: Insects and seeds mostly found on the ground.

NEST: Lichen-camouflaged cup in crotch of tree or bush.

The chaffinch is one of the commonest birds in the British Isles with a total population estimated at about 7 million pairs. Blackbird numbers are about the same. Wrens may sometimes reach around 10 million pairs but numbers drop dramatically after severe winters.

ROBIN

IDENTIFICATION: Male and female look identical with red breast, round body and characteristic upright stance. Young birds are brown all over with lighter speckling but share their parents' distinctive shape and carriage.

FLIGHT: Uniform mid brown wings, back and tail without markings

SEASON: All year. Males and females defend separate territories in winter.

VOICE: A charming song of deliberately spaced, unhurried notes with a unique tone. Both sexes sing in autumn when their songs have a softly melancholy quality, as if lamenting summer's end.

HABITAT: Woods, scrub, gardens, big hedges. Needs both shrub cover and open ground on which to feed.

FOOD: Mostly small invertebrates.

NEST: Concealed in a hole or cavity, usually low down.

The robin's readiness to perch confidingly beside you is less due to friendliness than you might think. In the primaeval forests of prehistoric Britain robins probably followed wild cattle and pigs to peck up insects and worms disturbed by hooves or rooting snouts. By digging your garden you provide much the same helpful service.

BULLFINCH
Length: 15cm
Male

CHAFFINCH
Length: 16cm
Male

Female

ROBIN
Length: 14cm

Useful Addresses:

The Wildlife Trust (Beds and Cambs)
5 Fulbourn Manor
Fulbourn
Cambridge
CB1 5BN

Berks, Bucks and Oxon Naturalists' Trust Limited
3 Church Cowley Road
Rose Hill
Oxford
OX4 3JR

Essex Naturalists Trust
Fingringhoe Wick Nature Reserve
South Green Road
Fingringhoe
Colchester
CO5 7DN

Hertfordshire and Middlesex Wildlife Trust
Grebe House
St Michaels Street
St Albans
Hertfordshire
AL3 4SN

Leicestershire and Rutland Trust for Nature Conservation
1 West Street
Leicester
LE1 6UU

Lincolnshire Trust for Nature Conservation
The Manor House
Alford
Lincs
LN13 9DL

Norfolk Naturalists Trust
72 Cathedral Close
Norwich
NR1 4DF

Northamptonshire Wildlife Trust
Lings House
Billing Lings
Northampton
NN3 4BE

Nottinghamshire Wildlife Trust
310 Sneinton Dale
Nottingham
NG3 7DN

Suffolk Wildlife Trust
Park Cottage
Main Road
Saxmundham
IP17 1DQ

The Royal Society for the Protection of Birds
Headquarters
The Lodge
Sandy, Beds
SG19 2DL

RSPB
(Thames and Chiltern)
The Lodge
Sandy
Bedfordshire
SG19 2DL

RSPB (East Anglia)
97 Yarmouth Road
Thorpe St Andrew
Norwich
NR7 0HF

RSPB (East Midlands)
12 Guildhall Street
Lincoln
LN1 1TT

British Trust for Ornithology
The Nunnery
Nunnery Place
Thetford
Norfolk
IP24 2PU

Wildfowl and Wetlands Trust
Slimbridge
Glos
GL2 7BT

The Tourist Information Centre
Rutland Water
Oakham
Leics
Tel. (078086) 321

Anglian Water
Eastern Division
Yare House
62/64 Thorpe Road
Norwich
NR1 1SA
Tel. (0603) 225000

Anglian Water
Northern Division
Waterside House
Lincoln
LN2 5HA
Tel. (0522) 557000

Anglian Water
Southern Division
33 Sheepen Road
Colchester, Essex
CO3 3LB
Tel. (0206) 774000

Anglian Water
Western Division
North Street
Oundle
Peterborough
PE8 4AS
Tel. (0832) 276000

Alphabetical Bird Index

NOTES

NOTES